KNOX-JOHNSTON
ON SEAMANSHIP & SEAFARING

ROBIN KNOX-JOHNSTON

Lessons & experiences from the 50 years since the start
of his record breaking voyage

FERNHURST
BOOKS

First published in 2018 by Fernhurst Books Limited

The Windmill, Mill Lane, Harbury, Leamington Spa, Warwickshire, CV33 9HP, UK.
Tel: +44 (0) 1926 337488 | www.fernhurstbooks.com

A catalogue record for this book is available from the British Library
ISBN 978-1-912177-14-1

Front cover photographs © Matthew Dickens and Bill Rowntree / PPL
Back cover photograph © Bob Aylott

Edited by Gill Pearson
Designed & typeset by Daniel Stephen
Printed in the UK by TJ International Ltd, Padstow, Cornwall

CONTENTS

Part Two: Seafaring   119

FOREWORD

ALEX THOMSON REFLECTS ON SIR ROBIN'S CONTRIBUTION

Sir Robin Knox-Johnston has been my boss, my mentor and a close friend.

He selected me to be a skipper in the 1998 Clipper Race after a 2-month trial sail as his first mate on an expedition to Greenland with Sir Chris Bonnington. Despite being just 24 / 25 years old Robin selected me as a skipper in the Round the World Race when I had yet to even cross the Atlantic, let alone circumnavigate the globe. If I had failed in that race, the responsibility would have landed firmly on Robin's shoulders. He never shared with me the personal risk he took with that decision and I did not realise until after the event, but if were not for him I would never have embarked on the journey I am now on.

Since then, we have remained close, with both our businesses based in Gosport, and I have even had the fun of sailing and zipping around in ZapCats with him.

I may have sailed faster than him single-handed, non-stop around the world, but such times will always be transitory – someone will always, eventually, go faster. He has the one record which no one else can have – he was the first! None of us professional sailors with our ultra-light and fast craft, now with foils, can ever take that away from him.

To be the first to do something like this takes incredible courage and perseverance. Many doubted it would be possible and, given that he was the only one to complete that first race, it very nearly wasn't possible at that time. The boat and equipment he had were so primitive compared to what we use today and yet he succeeded when everyone else failed. It is easy to forget that he also built this boat with his own hands – something inconceivable today.

It took immense seamanship to complete that voyage, and he learnt as he went around. He has continued to sail and continued to learn, not least through training hundreds of amateurs to complete a round-the-world voyage. That is what makes this book so exciting – it contains many of the things that Robin has learned in the years since he set off from Falmouth in 1968. Anyone who ventures to sea would be wise to take advantage of the seamanship lessons that Robin has learned.

However, anyone who has met Robin also knows that he is not just a wise old seaman – he is also great fun and lives life to the full. This shows in the pieces on seafaring in this book where he tells of some of his favourite boats, races and places he has visited – always with a twinkle in his eye! They are a joy to read and remind us that sailing is primarily a fun activity, to be enjoyed!

As we approach the 50th anniversary of Robin's epic first non-stop solo circumnavigation I salute him and urge you to read this book – both to learn and to be entertained.

Alex Thomson
June 2018

INTRODUCTION

SIR ROBIN REMINISCES ON THE PAST 50 YEARS

50 years seem to have passed so quickly, but when I look at my sport I realise that a great deal has happened in that time. It can be compared to the differences in aviation between the time of the Wright Brothers and the arrival of Concorde.

Yachting generally in the 1950's and 60's was seeing a large increase, although the number of international trans-oceanic voyages was still small. The introduction of glues used in aircraft production during the previous war for wooden aircraft created a DIY boatbuilding revolution. Dinghies could now be made at home using plywood, and special kits could be bought for dinghies such as the Wayfarer, Cartop, later called the Heron, and the simple, cheap and numerous Mirrors, of which more than 70,000 were built.

Access to cheap boats greatly increased the numbers of people involved in the sport and removed the stigma that yachting was a sport only available to the wealthy. Glass Reinforced Plastic (GRP), invented in the USA in the 1930s, began to have an effect on yacht construction in Britain in the 1950s. A precise female mould, into which glass mat or fibres bonded by resin are put, did not require the skills of a highly trained shipwright. Less skilled labour could be used using the same mould again and again. Soon larger yachts were being built using GRP.

Carbon fibre is almost de rigueur for racing boats these days, a material that was just being tried for aircraft half a century before and its use for spars has had a profound impact, allowing for much less weight in rigs and therefore an increase in stability, or a less heavy keel, which means a lighter and so faster boat. Whilst stainless steel rigging wires are still common, man-made fibres are making a big impact today.

Who could have foreseen foiling yachts? Multi-hulls have been around in Europe from the seventeenth century, although used centuries before in Asia and the Pacific, but they only really began to show their paces when the new materials came in. But now we can lift the hulls clear of the water and the lack of friction has created speeds unthought of just a decade ago. The first time I saw a Moth dinghy foiling I thought I was hallucinating until it whizzed past with hardly a sound. Fascinating for me, exciting for the sailor aboard.

The increase in the numbers of boat ownership has led to a huge change in where we keep our boats. A few marinas existed in the 1960s, but most boats were moored by their anchors or on swinging moorings and a lot of these moorings were controlled by Yacht Clubs. Having never sailed in the UK before, I returned from the Golden Globe Race and automatically assumed that, on arrival at a destination, one tied up to a yacht club and made oneself known, as in India and Africa. I quickly leant that this was only available to members of the club in the UK!

Sailing around the world 50 years ago, the boat was most likely constructed of wood, the sails of Dacron, rigging of plough wire, food in tins and water in tanks or caught in the sails from rainfall. Long voyages were still a rarity. The first of the modern trans-Atlantic races did not take place until 1960 and voyages around the world were cruises until Francis Chichester circumnavigated with one stop in 1966/7.

One problem at the time was that keeping sufficient provisions edible for long periods was not possible. Tins, the only way to store food, had to be protected as the voyage might last months. This meant coding them with paint, then removing their paper labels (which loved blocking bilge pumps) and finally coating them with varnish to keep them from rusting. Eggs needed to be varnished or coated with Vaseline and no vegetables lasted more than a couple of months. Most boats had leaks and, even if they were dry, the damp atmosphere quickly attacked fruit and vegetables and the tin coating, and eventually caused an inevitable hole which ruined the contents. The light-weight freeze-dried foods we can buy today were not even a dream.

Clothing was nothing like the smart sailing gear that is now available. Being permanently damp was the norm, especially in places like the Southern Ocean. One way I found of getting rid of the salt that inevitably built up in one's clothes was to tow them astern in the sea. This reduced the density of salt at least! The Yellow Wellies had not arrived on the scene: agricultural Wellington boots were more the norm. Towards the end of my ten-and-a-half-month non-stop circumnavigation, my foul weather gear had lost all its waterproofing and was letting in so much water that I cut holes in the bottom of the boots to let the water out! It kept out most of the wind though.

Compass bearings of identifiable objects ashore were the main means of coastal navigation and radio direction bearings offshore if a Direction Finder was carried. In oceanic voyages you relied on Dead Reckoning and using a sextant when the sun, moon or stars could be seen (which meant no position was possible at night when the horizon could not be seen to act as the datum for taking altitudes).

Not many boats carry a proper chronometer these days but they were essential then. The rate of change of a chronometer, whether it was increasing or decreasing its error, was a vital piece of information, occasionally checked by medium frequency transmissions if a single-side band radio was installed. Or a small transistor radio could pick up broadcasts when close to land. A second out can mean a mile of error and after a couple of months across an ocean, if the chronometer drifted, land could arrive unexpectedly!

Communication was by radio, usually low powered, and contacting a shore station to make a call could take hours. If the liner Queen Elizabeth or HMS Ark Royal was trying to contact the shore station at the same time, unless you could get through on a different frequency, you might just as well switch off for a few hours as the power of their radios swamped the yacht's puny signal. Conversations on the radio tended to be stilted as you knew that all the other ships awaiting their turn were listening in to what you said. VHF radios were almost unknown, but one could use an Aldis signal lamp to ask a ship to report one's position if one was in sight, as most ships were able to communicate using Morse code.

Without a radio or sighting of a ship, a yacht could go unreported for months. In my case no one knew where I was after I passed New Zealand until I ran into a line of ships near the Azores 4½ months later. The comment from well-meaning people "Weren't you worried when you were missing?" was countered by the honest answer that I was not missing as I knew where I was, I just had no means of telling anyone!

Nor, of course, could I have called for help if I had got into trouble which meant one had to be more self-reliant.

Since then, of course, ocean sailing has been totally changed by the introduction of satellites. These have revolutionised communications and made sailing a lot safer. The tracking devices that are automatically updating the boat's position via satellite mean that people ashore know exactly where the boat is and, if the boat has an emergency, it can transmit a signal it knows will get through regardless of low power and busy radio shore stations.

In shorter ranges, in place of the trusty Aldis signal light and the necessary knowledge of Morse code, we now have VHF radios which anyone can use since the Government restrictions on radio transmitters have been removed. And a simple addition to the VHF radio allows the connection to the Automatic Identification System (AIS): one of the greatest boons to the modern sailor. It means that not only can a boat see what ships are in range, what course and speed they are making and what type, but also the other vessels will pick up your own boat's signal, greatly improving the chances of being seen and reducing the risk of being run down. Single Side Band (SSB) radios are now rarely used for long distance communications.

No one could have imagined the Global Positioning System (GPS) which can fix a boat's position to within a couple of metres every 3 seconds. It has been a huge boon to yachting as it allows people to navigate with great accuracy without the need to learn the use of spherical trigonometry to calculate a sight reduction from sextant readings.

People who would never have considered a long voyage 50 years ago can now navigate oceans with confidence and racing boats do not need a navigator, replacing that position with a meteorologist. And before some traditionalists say "But what happens if the satellites are switched off?", think about the aircraft flying all over the world without sextants and probably with pilots who would not know how to use them. It might be an idea though, to carry a small battery-operated GPS receiver as a standby in case the main set breaks down!

Tactics and strategy have changed radically as a result of this instant access to information. Whereas 50 years ago the only weather information available was transmitted in Morse code, we have programmes now that bring us up-to-date weather every 6 hours to a relatively simple computerised plotter, and can provide predictions ten days in advance. This allows tactical decisions to be made to place the boat where the winds are likely to be most advantageous. Voyages have become faster as a result of being able to choose the weather, and bad weather can be more easily avoided. This is a huge advance on being reliant upon a Barometer, the wind direction and strength and the cloud formations which was all we had in 1968.

On the negative side, the wonderful Admiral's Cup series between international teams of three boats was killed off by the arrival of professional crews. The early Whitbread Races went the same way as enthusiastic volunteers were replaced by mercenaries for what became the Volvo. It can be argued that wealthy men who owned boats have been replaced by even wealthier sponsors which has brought money into the sport, and certainly the costs of modern offshore and ocean racing boats mean that they are really only accessible to the wealthy or sponsors. But the Corinthian spirit that provided so much sporting atmosphere and camaraderie has suffered. The pathway to these events, which anyone could have aspired to join 40 years ago, has become almost inaccessible to the ordinary yachtsmen as a result.

One of the positive things that has happened has been the introduction of disabled sailing, an initiative supported by the Royal Yachting Association (RYA). Many of the special inventions that have made this possible have helped those with physical infirmities to compete on a level plain with everyone else. It is growing worldwide.

Another initiative, which has encouraged people to improve their knowledge, and therefore their safety, was in 1973 when the RYA took over the administration from the Board of Trade of the Yachtmaster scheme and management of training and delivery of exams leading to the qualification. It has run ever since and to guarantee the syllabus and integrity of the scheme and its examinations, the Maritime and Coastguard Agency, the successor to the Board of Trade, has a seat on the RYA / MCA Yachtmaster Qualification Panel. This has proved so successful that the RYA Yachtmaster Qualification is now accepted for commercial use in a range of countries outside the UK.

Coming soon we may see unmanned vessels crossing our oceans. Something unthinkable just a few years ago. It used to be that solo sailors were criticised for being unable to comply with Rule 5 of the collision regulations (the requirement to keep a lookout), but how long will it be before we can expect to see Rule 5 changed to suit commercial imperatives?

So much has happened in these past 50 years. One simple statistic really says it all. In fifty years the time for solo sailing around the world has gone from 312 days down to 42 days, an incredible improvement. Before this book has been on the shelves very long will someone fly around on foils even faster? Oh to be 50 years younger but with today's equipment!

Sir Robin Knox-Johnston
June 2018

PART ONE

SEAMANSHIP

SKILLS

"The sea is an alien environment and is often unpredictable and frightening. It can never be mastered completely, but experience does count."

Robin Knox-Johnston, June 2009

YOUR FIRST OCEAN PASSAGE

Preparing for your first ocean voyage requires a checklist for everything from sunscreen and underwear to specialist clothing and health products, the latter being the first consideration.

I am often asked for advice on what to look out for and what to take by people planning their first ocean passage. When watching a novice crew prepare for their first ocean crossing, it is very easy to get swept away by the enthusiasm, coupled with a certain amount of apprehension. However experienced a land traveller the crew might be, the first ocean crossing is an adventure, and must be prepared for properly.

The most important point to get across is the sad fact that there are no shops or hospitals in mid ocean. If you have forgotten something you are going to have to do without it until the next port is reached, perhaps two or three weeks away or longer. So try to think of everything that you might usually require over a month and, if unsure, spend a day with a notepad from waking to going to bed that night and note down everything you use, from toothpaste to sunglasses, sun cream to spare socks, towels to underwear.

Health has to be the first consideration. For example a cold is an inconvenience that can be overcome, but any residual disease or injury that might cause a person to have to be confined to their bunk is an imposition on the rest of the crew. It is not just the nursing that may be required, it is the increase in work for everyone else because one person is not available to do their share. With a small crew this will lead to tiredness and frustration and this often happens at the beginning of a voyage when some of the crew may be suffering from sea sickness for a few days.

Obviously the skipper must be told of any special medical issues or allergies that might affect a crew or which require regular medication. Once at sea, although there is a good medical service by radio that can be contacted via the coastguard, unless there is a doctor aboard, most medical treatment is going to be limited to first aid. Many problems that would have made a long voyage an impossibility even 50 years ago can now be controlled by drugs, but it is vital to ensure that a sufficient quantity of the proper drugs are being carried and being stored correctly. Some drugs need to be kept cool, and this can present difficulties on a yacht unless it has a reliable fridge. This applies to what an individual might require on a regular basis just as much as the need for a good supply of appropriate treatments for whatever else might develop. In mid ocean, well out of range of helicopters, evacuation may not be a speedy option and it has to be remembered that only liners and cruise ships carry doctors among merchant vessels.

Clothing is always an issue. The old adage was: 'if you think you have enough sweaters, pack one more.' These days we have advanced technically and there are a variety of warm breathable, water dispelling items available. Yachts do not have a lot of dry space and, if the yacht is racing, the skipper will want to keep the weight down so one bag may be all that is allowed. Common sense applies here. If the voyage is to a cold area, make sure that you have good warm weather underclothes; if it is to a hot zone, shorts and sun protection. Remember that the risk of sunburn doubles at sea as, in addition to the direct rays of the sun, there are the reflected rays off the sea's surface. To avoid burning take the sun in easy stages to build up the tan. While washing facilities are probably limited, do not take too much clothing and keep some clean clothes aside for arrival, preferably sealed in a plastic bag. A good way to avoid creases in items like trousers is to roll them up when stowing them.

Look at the requirements of the countries that will be visited. Some demand visas, the US does if you arrive by yacht for example. Others may require vaccinations.

Finally, if you are the first volunteer to do the hard or dirty jobs before being asked, you will be a popular crew member and invited again.

LEARNING FROM OTHERS

Improving your seamanship, and building your confidence, should be a shared learning experience.

I wonder how many families are put off cruising because of a lack of confidence in their ability to handle their boat and sail it safely? Buying the boat is the easy part of sailing, anyone can do it if they have the money or can obtain a mortgage. But taking a family out into coastal waters can be a frightening responsibility for someone who may have the relevant RYA qualification but lacks a lot of experience. This can lead to stress, which often shows up as irritability. It creates a far from enjoyable outing for everyone as a result.

Of course an experienced friend could always help. Going out with an experienced skipper can help to fill in the areas of insecurity and build confidence. The Liverpool Yacht Club are asking experienced sailors to help the less experienced for this purpose. Sailing with someone who knows what they are doing is an opportunity to learn quietly and free from embarrassment. Of course there will be mistakes, but it is these that we remember far better than something we have learned theoretically. The more mistakes made in the early days, the fewer we are likely to make thereafter, but hopefully an experienced companion will limit them.

Seamanship has always been a hands-on discipline. We learn it far better practically, by doing things. And repetition, although it can be boring, ensures that we automatically do the right thing in an emergency. Just think about bringing a boat alongside a berth or onto a mooring. You can read how to do it, but that is rather like learning to swim from a book.

It is practice that teaches you what to look out for, like the wind and the tide effects and the transverse thrust of the propeller.

To reach the stage where we feel confident enough to handle a boat, and the unexpected situations that will arise, requires experience, and that means time afloat, the more the better. Remove the nervousness and provide encouragement and our sport will expand. When the skipper feels confident to sail around the coast they might want to go further afield, but an ocean crossing is a far greater challenge than cruising to the continent. But it is not out of reach. Here the ARC has shown us the way in many respects. This organised cruise in company across the Atlantic provides boats and crews with the feeling of security they seek because they know they are part of a fleet where the members communicate with each other, and provide mutual support. In the event of an emergency they know that help is likely to be available quite quickly. An Atlantic crossing may seem an ambitious undertaking for the weekend sailor, but the ARC has shown that it can be achieved.

This excellent example can be followed on a smaller scale. There must be thousands of boat owners who would use their boats more often if more shared events were organised. We call them rallies and they are usually organised by clubs. Perhaps clubs who do not organise them should consider this. It's not just the sail in company and the assurance that brings, or the anchoring safely, or the use of dinghies, it's the exchange of information, the comparisons of how well the boats sail on different points, even learning the proper use of the VHF radio (fines for anyone who says "over and OUT"!). Perhaps rowing races for the youngsters to develop their skills, or other activities, like another much neglected skill, how to throw a heaving line. And of course there is the socialising, which is why one joins a club in the first place. Confidence comes from learning and one of the best ways to learn is by sharing an experience and swapping notes.

So to encourage more people to use their boats with confidence first we have to get people to join a club and participate in rallies. A lot of clubs have seen a decline in their membership in recent years so it is time to come up with new initiatives. This year the Little Ship Club has decided to invite people to join in one of their several rallies as a non-member. Hopefully this will be taken up by non-members as an opportunity to sail further afield, and, perhaps, encourage them to join the club.

GAINING EXPERIENCE IS VITAL

Forget the chit of paper which makes its holder a Yachtmaster after 16 weeks in a sailing school; long hours of sea-time and the school of hard knocks are the makings of a good sailor.

Recent articles in this magazine about fast-track yachting qualifications worry me for two reasons: first is that people will think the holder of the qualification is experienced; second that the holder themselves will think they are ready to take charge of a boat.

You can gain the piece of paper which accredits you with 2,500 miles of sailing on a course where you are never unsupervised. However, if we want the Yachtmaster (Ocean) to really mean something we have to make it more demanding.

I have been selecting skippers for the Clipper race around the world for the last few months. All have to hold an RYA Yachtmaster Certificate with Commercial endorsements, as required by the authorities, in this case the MCA, and without holding this qualification skippers cannot take charge of a boat used for commercial activities. But achieving this qualification in a few months, which will satisfy government requirements, is no way to measure a candidate's ability to take charge of a yacht and sail it around the world.

I have reached the point where I take the written qualifications for granted and then try to find out just how experienced the candidate really is. I want to know how many miles of ocean sailing they have actually done and in what capacity they have done it. Have they experience of dealing with a crew far from land, where people may develop all sorts of worries or even change character?

I am reassured if they have spent plenty of time at sea. After that you just have to go on your gut feeling for people and there is no better way of making this judgement than by taking them to sea and spending a few days sailing; it is very hard to keep up an act for three or four days, especially when the working hours are unsocial.

A captain I sailed with in the Navy who had worked as an instructor in Dartmouth told me that the best test of a cadet he was unsure of was to take them to sea in a yacht. The same theory ought to be applied when selecting crew. Do you want to take them on spec, untested, or are you going to take them out for a few days just to make sure they are capable and can fit in?

We gain experience by watching someone, understudying them and working with them. Mistakes will be made, but as Napoleon once said: "A man who never makes a mistake never makes anything." We learn from our mistakes and the longer we spend at sea, the more mistakes we will make (or see being made), therefore if we apply what we have learned, the better and safer sailors we become. Time on the job is what matters – in this case time at sea.

We learn from our mistakes because we are interested – embarrassed, perhaps – or because we have frightened ourselves and we apply that experience to all our future actions. Having a qualification is fine, it shows a knowledge of the theory, but would you really want to cross the Atlantic with a skipper who had never sailed across an ocean before?

But it seems that pieces of paper count these days, not experience and ability. Paper is simple to assess; you either have it or you don't. However, making a judgement requires experience and knowledge and that is subjective. You would not expect two people to come to exactly the same conclusion of a person's character and officialdom prefers certainties.

The only way to introduce a certainty that officialdom can cope with is to introduce a minimum amount of sea-time before a candidate can sit for an examination for a specific certificate, as is the case with Merchant Navy qualifications. The eight years' foreign-going sea-time required before someone can sit for a Class 1 Masters certificate is excessive for yachtsmen. A Class 3 certificate requires four years as a cadet or seaman, so an Ocean Yachtmaster should probably have a minimum of two years' proven sea-time, including ocean experience and time as skipper of a yacht in UK and European waters.

If we want the RYA qualifications to mean something, then they have to be recognised and acknowledged by all in yachting as being of a high standard. That way they attract respect from the industry and generate pride in their holders.

DEVELOPING A HARMONIOUS CREW

It's a tough job being a skipper. Not only is he responsible for the boat and all the legal issues, but he must deal efficiently with a diverse and not always harmonious crew.

The dynamics of a crew at sea are a subject that has not been well explored. The key person is the skipper and it is a greater responsibility than most people appreciate. It includes the safe operation of the yacht as well as the safety of the crew and some legal liability if things go wrong. The sea is an alien environment and is often unpredictable and frightening. It can never be mastered completely, but experience does count.

Then there are all the rules that cover the interaction with other vessels, port rules as you depart and arrive and how to call or respond in an emergency. There is also the vital issue of the provision of good meals, watch keeping, and so on.

Into this strange pressure cooker we throw people, but not professional sailors, ordinary people whose normal job employs them five days a week and for whom sailing is a leisure pastime. They come in all types, backgrounds and levels of experience. Some are easy going, some argumentative. Some are hard workers and some will skive. Some fit, some not. Some pick up things quickly and with others you wonder if they can ever learn anything useful. Somehow such a polyglot mix has to be welded into an effective and happy crew and this is the skipper's job.

It is easier to keep a crew happy and motivated when the skipper is the most experienced member of the crew and also the owner, but sometimes this is not the case. Ownership is not necessarily such a strong support for authority when the boat is out at sea and people feel frightened. The worst scenario is where a crew member is more experienced than the skipper and lets it be known. This will lead to challenges to authority, disruption as people take sides and confusion in a real emergency.

One of the most dangerous crew members will be the person who thinks they have learnt everything early on and starts to pontificate. This occasionally happens with Clipper crews and the answer is simple: move onto subjects that the person has not learnt, so they begin to appreciate they are not as knowledgeable as they had thought and those they are trying to impress can see it. Experienced skippers have less of a problem as the wide and varied knowledge they have built up over the years will ensure they can always keep ahead.

The best method is to start by expecting all the crew to learn as the voyage progresses and showing them how much there is to learn. The Almanac provides plenty of subjects that need to be mastered – just studying the collision regulations can keep people occupied for weeks!

But what happens if a conflict develops between two crew members? It so easily happens. Someone takes a dislike to the way another clears their throat, or leaves the gear lying around and the bickering starts. It takes time for people to learn to accept another's foibles, but there can be a lot of unrest until this happens. Soon the whole crew is suffering and it has to be stopped.

We had this on *Condor* in the Whitbread Round the World Race in 1977, when one crew from each watch took a dislike to each other. Quiet talking achieved nothing so in desperation I decided to spend a day picking on them both. First I told the mate, Peter Blake, who was as frustrated as I was, so if my plan failed he could pick up the pieces!

Throughout the day, whenever the watch on deck made a mistake, I blamed the person who was having trouble with his fellow crew member. I watched them respond with surprise, then anger and finally hatred of me. By the evening, when we collected in the cockpit to go through the day and prepare for the night, they both chose to sit as far away from me as possible – but they were talking to each other! They had found something in common, their dislike of me. The good news was that it broke their dislike of each other and, after a few days, they stopped disliking me too.

That was extreme, and I am sure is not taught by Human Resources or modern management courses, but we were 20 days from the next stop, nothing else had worked and I needed a crew to work together without hesitation.

MINIMISING ACCIDENTS

Accidents will happen, but if you've safety-proofed the boat and acclimatised new crew to what they're in for, you can really help to reduce the risks of serious injury.

Accidents to boats from collisions, grounding, fire, hull damage and the like always attract attention. As well as noting any drama that may make the news, most of us will read up a rather more carefully prepared account to see what lessons might be learnt. Personal accidents such as someone falling overside, or being injured by a boom might make the news, especially if they are fatal or require evacuation, but how many accidents take place on yachts that never warrant this attention, but cause injury to crew members?

If we look at a yacht, the potential for accidents is high. Boats tend to have narrow access between deck and cabin with steep, small-stepped ladders, sometimes varnished and without a gripping tread. On deck, booms and ropes are flying around when tacking or if the boat goes onto her side in a squall. A person losing their grip when a large wave strikes or the boat pounds heavily is in a potentially dangerous situation because losing balance can cause them to stumble across a heeling cabin or deck, resulting in a jar at best, bruises or even a broken limb at worst.

In commercial shipping, slips, trips and falls are the most common cause of injuries and I suspect the same applies on yachts. We can deal with some of the common causes, many of which will exist when a boat has just been delivered. Sharp corners on furniture or deckhouses are like hungry rocks, awaiting the arrival of the unwary. Isolated bolts on deck await the unshoe'd toe.

We can put covers on bolts, cut solid rubber balls in half, hollow out the centre to make space for the bolt head and use Evomastic sealant to secure them to the deck over bolts and on top of any exposed bolts down below. I was once flung across the cabin of a large boat. I put out my hand to check myself and punctured my hand when it hit an exposed bolt.

Elsewhere, we can put anti-skid material on steps and we can work our way around a boat checking whether we have sufficient handholds and in the right places. Look for the distance it is possible to fall if the boat goes over. The larger the boat and wider the cabin, the greater the potential for injury. A glistening gelcoated deck may look lovely in the marina, but be a serious slip risk once wet and heeled at sea.

A crew being rushed or pressured to do a job quickly, as happens when racing, can be particularly vulnerable. No one wants to be the person who slowed down a manoeuvre so attention is on getting the job done, not on what would be normal safety procedures. Training can reduce these risks by making the job so familiar that it becomes automatic, thus speeding up the actual performance of the evolution which removes the pressure to hurry. A small mistake in carrying out a task is likely to lose far more time than is lost by someone taking their time to do it safely.

In the end, though, it all comes down to experience and briefing of new crew. I have always thought it self-defeating to take new crew out in anything above a Force 4 because they are going to wonder – quite reasonably – what on earth is happening to them and how safe they are and probably lose their enthusiasm.

Things such as tearing their new oilskins on an uncovered bolt is discouraging. Allow them to get used to the unfamiliar sensation of their 'home' heeling over and understand movement is going to be slower because it is not so easy to move about a heeled boat. They must not feel they have to stand in the wind, trying to balance on unsteady legs because Gregory Peck did in some film. Remind them to keep their centre of gravity low and not to be afraid of crawling around if they feel insecure.

The most important point is to build confidence in this new and unfamiliar world. The old sailing ship adage of one hand for yourself and one for the ship is just as applicable on a small yacht as it was on the topmast yard of a square rigger rounding Cape Horn.

MAKING IT SAFE BELOW

Dramatic accidents on deck garner all the headlines, but remember that below decks can be just as hazardous when the boat is tossing about and lurching unexpectedly.

Accidents below decks tend to receive less attention than those on deck, but they can be serious, and more so the larger the boat. This might seem contradictory – you would expect a small boat to be thrown about more and thus cause more damage to its crew. However, although the larger boat might not be thrown about as much – and that is relative to the size of the waves anyway – the space below is greater so that, when the boat is slammed or knocked down, there is a greater distance to be thrown before coming up against something, so the blow will be harder.

There are things that can be done to limit the injuries. It is obvious to everyone that, if your hands are free, you can put them out to try to lessen the impact, or grab a handhold (if there is one in immediate reach). But if you are carrying something, that might not be possible.

This is particularly relevant when climbing into or out of your foulweather gear when your hands or legs can be trapped just as the boat lurches. Ideally, crew coming on deck should be helped into their gear to avoid this. The alternative is to brace yourself in a fore and aft passageway so you are leaning on the lee side and have no distance to topple. (Once dressed and ready to go on deck, do not forget to clip on your safety harness before you exit the companionway.)

The only really effective method of finding where to put handholds is to take the boat to sea, get her well heeled and then try to move around below decks. Where you have a problem finding something to provide support, make a note to put a handhold there. This won't just make movement safer, it also makes it a lot faster.

Companionway steps are another risk, especially when wet and slippery. To avoid tumbling down them make sure there are good handholds and keep holding them until your boots are firmly on the cabin sole.

As on deck, keep your weight low whenever possible. You are less likely to topple if you are sitting rather than standing. But whereas you should try to keep to the high side when manoeuvring along the weather deck, the opposite applies below. Stick to the low side as you will have less far to fall.

The galley is always a source of danger. It is surprising how many larger yachts will have the stove positioned where the cook is facing fore or aft with nothing to hold them from toppling sideways across the boat if it lurches suddenly. A safety belt / harness is one solution, but the problem can be avoided if the stove is placed so that there are fore and aft bulkheads to restrict the distance a person can fall sideways.

This is where burns are a risk. Putting meals in pressure cookers helps as they have a lid and if they fall from the stove the contents do not get thrown out, but a stove still needs to be properly gimballed.

On many stoves the weight of one heavy saucepan or kettle can cause it to list and, if fiddles are not fitted, the pan can slide across and overturn. The answer is to avoid having pans that are too heavy and not to overfill them. Using two saucepans instead of one can make a lot of sense in rough conditions.

Probably the most nasty bruises and rib fractures are caused by crew falling from their bunks. Obviously the risk is less if you are in a lower bunk, but self-evidently not everyone can have this berth, some have to be in the upper bunks. Having decent and well-secured leecloths will prevent most accidental tumbles. The upper berths on the weather side are particularly vulnerable when climbing in or out – this can sometimes be almost as difficult as climbing the futtock shrouds on a square rigger!

An injured crew is not just one less hand to help with the work; it is someone who must be cared for. Most of all it is someone you know who is suffering and that can put a damper on the morale of any voyage.

REVIEWING SAFETY PROCEDURES & EQUIPMENT

The New Year is a good time to reconsider your safety procedures and ensure that all your crew are properly trained and qualified.

Sixteen bells rung out by the youngest member of the crew traditionally announces the beginning of a New Year aboard a ship. It's a pleasant custom, enjoyed with a degree of anticipation by a crew, none of whom will be more than four hours from a spell of duty.

At home the bell is silent, in respect of the neighbours if you happen to have taken it off the boat, and most of us can look forward to a night in our beds, but this does not stop us going through the enjoyable motions of making resolutions and plans for the coming season.

It is no accident that sailing is one the safest sports, far safer than mountaineering or riding, for example, despite the fact that most crews are unsupervised amateurs in a dangerous environment.

We are brought up to consider that safety is the very essence of good seamanship and there can be no higher praise than to have someone say of any sailor that he is a good sailor. We have created the right culture of safety in our sport and it is something of which we can all be very proud.

Few other sports have their training so well organised. At any one time there are over 100,000 people in training for an RYA certificate of some sort in recognised courses around the country. The fact that there is no compulsion to take such courses, since there are no mandatory requirements for the average boat owner, only makes this figure seem more remarkable.

But, although it may seem impressive, in fact it is not nearly high enough. There are estimated to be a minimum of 2½ million people who relax in boats, but this may be on the low side. If only one in every 25 participants is bothering to take a course to improve themselves, then there is a strong need to promote education further.

The Sports Council has estimated that there are 800,000 craft of all types in Britain, 250,000 of which are over 7.5m in length and 80,000 registered in one form or another for foreign travel. Perhaps all the larger ones have people aboard who have bothered to study how to control a boat at sea, manoeuvre safely to avoid inconveniencing others, work out a tide, fix a position, deal with a Man Overboard situation, fire or a medical emergency – but it is fair to suppose that they haven't.

Listening to a distress call where the caller to the Coastguard didn't know where he was, could not even give a recognisable description of his position (although it was in the Solent), and was unable even to answer the question as to whether the craft had a single keel or was a bilge keeler, may be the sad exception, but just one case like this damages the reputation of all sailors.

That may be a particularly poor case, although the Coastguard will tell of plenty similar, but however well qualified we are, safety is not something that can be taken for granted. Just because we passed an examination a few years ago and have a piece of paper to prove it does not mean we need no longer keep abreast of developments, or ensure that we are maintaining our own standards.

So the New Year is not a bad time to hold an audit, consider the equipment carried aboard, test the safety procedures, reread the regulations for preventing collision at sea – just to remind ourselves of their meanings – and the instructions to the Almanacs, since knowledge of where to find information can save vital minutes.

It only takes a few hours, a small price to pay for your contribution to keeping our sport safe, not to mention an increase in self-confidence. Better still, talk about it in order to increase the pressure on those who have not bothered to obtain a qualification and protect the reputation of our sport.

TAKING HEED OF THE WEATHER FORECAST

When a predicted Force 9 that cancelled a passage fails to appear, it's hugely tempting to treat future forecasts with scepticism, but discretion remains the better part of valour.

Weather forecasts are a highly perishable commodity. While the synopsis is based on the most up-to-date information available, as we all know the meteorological situation can change very quickly. Meteorologists have to react just as swiftly to these changes. Their sources are ships at sea and land stations, which report their current situation, plus the impressive long-range information gleaned from high-tech satellites and assessed by an expensive Cray computer.

Nevertheless, forecasting remains a black art. Such is the number of variables to consider, the best computers in the world running the finest weather model programs available can still end up predicting the weather incorrectly. Small wonder, then, that forecasters tend to err on the side of caution and suggest the worst situation. If they risked giving anything less they would be subject to severe criticism at best and accused of risking lives or possibly even blamed for the deaths of seamen at worst. Who can blame them for playing safe?

So where does that leave the yachtsman? We know forecasters predict the worst possible situation, so we know the weather might be less severe than predicted, but dare we go to sea? Suppose we assume the forecast is an exaggeration, but it turns out to be correct? If we set sail, we could be accused of being irresponsible. But we might get lucky and the weather prove comparatively benign. The question is can we take the risk?

We were proceeding down the Solent, heading for Brest from Cowes, when the Met' Office issued a gale warning for Portland. It did not fit in with the rather confusing weather information we had been receiving, not just from the Met' Office, but also that published on the internet by alternative sources. (One of my gripes is that the BBC does not provide reports from coastal stations with each forecast. Such hard information is invaluable when predicting weather.)

The previous forecast had given the weather for Wight, Portland and Plymouth as cyclonic becoming north-westerly 6-8, 9 at first in Portland.

The Coastguard radio station forecast, broadcast 20 minutes after the latest BBC prediction at 0535 simply repeated the midnight forecast; we assumed the operator had picked up the wrong piece of paper and not checked the time of issue. An hour after the gale warning, the BBC forecast broadcast at 1201 reported north-westerly 6-8, becoming 4 – there was no mention of the Force 9 mentioned an hour earlier.

But by that time we were firmly moored in Yarmouth. I had taken the view that with a Gale Force warning we would be unwise to continue our voyage for the time being and decided to wait for the 1754 forecast and a favourable tide. When it came, though, it made no mention of gales and was down to north-westerly Force 5-6, occasionally 7, so we sailed. We could probably have sailed quite safely six hours earlier and enjoyed a better tide as a result, but that was being wise after the event.

We have all faced this situation before. Opting to stay alongside because of a bad forecast can seem an easy way out; an excuse to avoid going to sea for what we know might be a rough and potentially dangerous voyage. How much better (and, we might add, more seamanlike) to stay alongside and blame the forecast.

But at the back of our minds is the thought that if we left now, assuming the forecast to be exaggerated, we could be making good progress towards the destination. We have a good craft, we know it well, we have been through gales before and although no gale is enjoyable we are confident we can handle safely the conditions being forecast.

Perhaps the present wind direction is going to change as well and if we delay our departure we will receive adverse winds, while if we go now, despite the forecast, the wind is favourable. So what do we do?

I take the view that a gale is something we can well expect to meet at sea when on a long voyage and provided we have sea room we can usually ride it out without serious danger.

However, going to sea when the Met' Office is forecasting gales is taking a risk, not least because we are sailing close to land. It only takes one foul-up – a halyard to jam or the engine to refuse to start, for example – to start a chain of events that results in a dangerous situation. That risk is simply not worth the gamble.

USING WAYPOINTS

Is basic navigation nous being lost when navigators put marks into their chart plotters as waypoints and then keep on sailing until they run into them?

Every year there are a number of incidents when boats hit navigation marks or other hazards because skippers have put their co-ordinates into a chart plotter or GPS and just kept sailing on the resulting bearing until the collision inevitably takes place.

I suppose they think they will see the mark at the last minute and then avoid it, although that becomes a bit dicey when it is dark or there is thick fog and you have no radar. Of course, keeping a proper lookout ought to enable a boat to avoid a collision, but at night an unlit buoy may not be the easiest thing to pick out.

This is not a new problem, but it is one that has arrived in relatively recent years with the introduction of electronic navigation aids. The moment radio beacons were fitted to buoys and light vessels, some boats would navigate on a bearing that led them straight towards a beacon and, if they did not alter course at the last minute, they almost inevitably hit them, especially in poor visibility when the range was difficult to estimate. In the days of manned light vessels, you can imagine how their crew must have hated a limited visibility forecast!

The dangers are so obvious, and the collisions so well reported, that it makes it all the more surprising that the perpetrators have not thought to lay off a safe distance from the mark and aim for that instead.

The trouble is that electronic navigation has made navigating so easy that the depth of basic knowledge is often no longer there. And that is where the problem really starts.

Electronic navigation is not 100 per cent reliable and some people still haven't got that message. GPS signals can be degraded, which will give a false idea of position, and the plotter might have an error.

We are constantly warned about the very real danger of applying positions derived from GPS to a chart that might have been made more than 100 years ago and has not yet been adjusted for the slight differences between the astronomically derived positions on the charts and the need to create a perfect sphere for GPS.

In some cases, particularly in the less frequented parts of the world, where the initial survey was not conducted to the standards of a Captain Cook, these differences can be large, although usually modern charts will give a warning if large errors are in existence.

With all these potential errors, it really ought to be a matter of course always to check the warning on a new chart when it is brought out onto the chart table.

I was using a chart plotter some 13 years ago while I was sailing in Greenland. At one point I was clearly in the middle of a fjord – I could tell from the mountains on either side – but the plotter was showing our position halfway up an adjacent mountain! This was clearly a surveying error, not surprising given the difficulties of accurate surveys in deep fjords, with high mountains on each side north of the Arctic Circle.

In this case, the error was obvious – fjords tend to be very deep and clear in the middle and, of course, in Greenland there is plenty of light in the summer. But when approaching a low-lying island, particularly at night and with no obvious visual references, or when the dead reckoning might be based on a poor departure or a rather old position fix, it makes sense to play safe.

A few seconds saved by cutting close into a mark that you cannot see and where the position is only indicated by a GPS fix are never going to compensate for an injury or death as a result of a damaged or sunk boat.

Now, all these potential errors in the system might make you think paradoxically that it is quite safe to put a buoy into the route plan as a waypoint – after all, if electronic navigation is not 100 per cent accurate then surely you are bound to miss it if you aim straight for it?

Well, Murphy's Law comes in here. The buoy position might be a little bit inaccurate and so might your GPS, but suppose both are accurate? You won't know until you get there and the first you find out about it is a savage crash and the sound of water pouring in.

OBEYING THE COLREGS

The sea has always had to be shared by all kinds of vessels, and in order to be safe as possible we must continue to respect each other's rights and obey the COLREGs.

Yachtsmen are constantly being told to keep clear of merchant shipping, quite rightly as, apart from anything else, the vessels are usually a lot larger. They also know that merchant ships are restricted when they approach a port and, therefore, need to be given space to manoeuvre – indeed most port bye-laws enforce this. But if yachts respect merchant vessels' limitations and try keep out of their way, merchant vessels should understand when yachts cannot manoeuvre easily at sea.

These thoughts are generated by two recent incidents. In both, the same yacht was under spinnaker in the North East Trades and had picked up the merchant vessel at about 12 miles on radar and plotted its progress. The watch leader was a recently retired tanker master and the skipper was also highly experienced. At a range of six miles in both incidents, the merchant ships were showing a CPA of less than a mile and so the VHF was used to try to establish contact and intentions. No response was received until the merchant ships were close enough for their names to be read.

In the first case the crew of the *Mar Adriana* said they had been plotting the yacht on radar and had intended to alter course but did not need to as the yacht altered first.

This was true. When the name could be seen. All hands had been called, the spinnaker handed and the yacht came up into the wind to cross the wake about half a mile astern. It was clear the ship's crew had no concept of a yacht's limited manoeuvrability under spinnaker and thus forced the yacht to take evasive action.

The second case is more worrying. Again, no response was received on the VHF so the yacht gybed to diverge. While gybing, another yacht was heard to challenge the *Iron Prince* and asked why it had not responded to the yacht's calls. This ship said that it too was tracking the yacht on the radar but had no intention of altering course.

When asked to alter a few degrees. In order to pass astern of the yacht and allow it to gybe and continue its course, the *Iron Prince* refused and the yacht was forced to sail on the wrong course for 40 minutes until the merchant vessel had eventually passed ahead. Again, there was no obvious understanding of the yacht's abilities to manoeuvre under spinnaker.

Some 35 years ago when I was watchkeeping on merchant ships, yachts were a rarity. There were many more merchant ships about though and they had less effective radar than are available today, so a proper lookout was kept by the Officer of the Watch as well as the lookouts.

Merchant ships have become a lot larger, their crews have reduced to about quarter of the numbers needed to man a smaller freighter 40 years ago and, from personal observation, you seldom see a lookout these days. But that does not give merchant ships the right of way, or the right to treat yachts as just a nuisance, and it is certainly not the legal situation.

The sea has always had to be shared and it was in order to create a safe framework to enable vessels to operate safely in close quarters situations that the COLREGs were developed. In both the above cases, the yacht, which was the standing-on vessel, compiled with Rule 17 which means she took action to avoid the risk of collision. Both the merchant ships were overtaking and therefore should have kept clear under Rules 8 and 13. Why didn't they do so?

In the open oceans there are few restrictions on the ability of merchant ships to manoeuvre, and to alter the course a few degrees to pass astern of a yacht is hardly a difficult operation – in fact, it is just a small turn of a knob by one person.

The yacht, on the other hand, cannot do a great deal. If it turns off downwind, sooner or later it will probably have to gybe and, if it hardens up, it increases the wind strength, perhaps beyond the safe limits for the sail which will have to be changed or be torn. Either of which requires crew to be on deck.

Perhaps we cannot expect watchkeepers on large vessels to fully appreciate the problems of manoeuvring a yacht under sail, but we ought to be able to expect some respect of the COLREGs.

STAYING CLEAR

Good sense and good seamanship go hand in hand when it comes to observing traffic rules in busy shipping channels. Robin observes from the other side.

Motoring up the Solent at 18 knots on a large liner puts a new perspective on the meaning of close quarters situation. What no doubt appears to be safe distance from the cockpit of a yacht looks dangerously close from the bridge of the QE2, but the most concern was caused by boats whose movements were difficult to interpret – those which were heading straight across the path or angling diagonally to cross it.

The QE2 is 72,000 tons and is not able to swerve in time to avoid something close ahead and, as the Captain pointed out (and he is a yachtsman), even if she did alter course, it would only threaten other small vessels to one side or the other which had been clear up to that point.

My immediate assumption was that yachtsmen were not aware of the local byelaws covering shipping in the Solent area, but examination of the log of the accompanying safety vessel indicated otherwise.

Most boats that were challenged admitted that they had heard there were rules although not all knew the details. Excuses given for getting in the way divided pretty evenly between:

- 'I was well clear' (in one case from a yacht 100m in front of an approaching container ship when the moving exclusion zone extended 1,000m ahead!)

- 'The ship was going faster than I realised and I thought I had time to get across'
- 'The wind went light' (so use the motor, please, sir!)
- 'I'm sorry'

For those 35,000 yachts that habitually use the Solent, there are some significant points to be appreciated. The first is that most of the ships coming out of the Port of Southampton, except the very large tankers, only slow down at the Prince Consort buoy if coming from the east, and almost at Calshot Spit if from the Needles.

They need to keep speed on in order to turn sharply at these two points and, once committed, cannot manoeuvre out of the way of yachts in the channel. Every yachtsman knows that if they want to turn sharply they need to put on high revs to direct a good wash against the rudder – well, this applies to giants as well.

The safety boats that now accompany vessels coming through the channels will tow becalmed yachts out of the way, but they rely on the intelligence and watchfulness of other boats to keep well clear. If there are a number of yachts becalmed in the channel there is going to be trouble, since there just won't be time to get them all.

The classic case of this was when the offshore racing fleet was becalmed and many kedged right in the channel, in the centre of the zone of concern. The container ship coming through had a simple choice: hit four ahead or three astern. It took the cheaper alternative!

There were, no doubt, some indignant yachtsmen as a result, but they only have themselves to blame. A tight dredged channel into a busy principal port is hardly an intelligent place to anchor and this is clear example where the Rules of the Road take precedence over the racing rules.

Surprisingly, on average, only three are hit each year, or perhaps that should be put the other way round, as on two occasions recently the yachts have rammed the ships. One was a sailing school boat which went bow first into the ship's side; the other was a small cruiser, out for the first time with new owners who could not get their engine started quickly enough.

They bounced down the side, damaging hull and rigging in the process, and were lucky enough to avoid serious difficulties at the stern where the propellers create a suction. Either way, it was a sad start to their new ownership.

This happened on a Sunday in early October, so the Solent was only moderately busy; it must be a nightmare during Cowes Week. The port authorities do have power to take owners who flout the rules to court, but thus has been very sparing so far.

If yachtsmen don't want a rash of summonses, the rule has to be: if you see a large vessel coming up the channel, get clear of the zone of concern in good time. It is both considerate and common sense – in other words good seamanship.

AVOIDING A COLLISION

A quick assessment of a vessel's course, speed and intentions is vital to avoid collision. Sir Robin finds it easier at night when navigation lights help with identification.

One of a seaman's most vital skills is collision avoidance. This becomes even more relevant when you are in a small boat and a collision is likely to result in the loss of the yacht and all her crew. The collision regulations or COLREGs are remarkably simple and straightforward when you consider the complexity of potential problems with traffic, particularly in crowded waters, and they have stood the test of time. They do depend upon one fundamental, however – the early sighting and speedy assessment of an approaching vessel's course, speed and intentions.

I have always found it far easier to discover what a vessel is doing at night. The navigation lights make its identification and course very clear – assuming there is good visibility of course. By day it can take a little longer to assess a vessel's course. Navigation lights have clearly defined arcs of visibility and, even if their ranges are still defined by the power of paraffin lanterns, this works to our benefit as in practice they are much more powerful and give far earlier identification.

The basic lights for vessels have not changed in years. The two masthead lights for vessels of more than 50m in length are clear and in good visibility the sidelights can be picked up early. The introduction of the red over green all-round masthead lights for a sailing vessel, one of the few additions in recent years, is a welcome contribution to safety.

Some concern has been expressed recently that, with the increased size of vessels on the oceans these days, two masthead lights are insufficient and vessels of more than 900ft in length should show a third. The contention is that it is sometimes difficult to judge whether there are one or two vessels approaching.

Personally I cannot see the point. In my view, the existing lights are easy enough to identify and introducing a third is more likely to lead to a watchkeeper thinking a second vessel is close by and there is gap to wriggle through – if they were stupid enough to want to go that close to a couple of large ships.

Tugs with long tows are an even more fertile subject for change. It is not always easy to see the towed barge or ship and, if that towline is long, as it will be in the ocean, the towline can be sufficiently behind for it to appear as a separate vessel.

Again it is usually easier to identify a tug with a tow at night as the three white masthead lights on the tug tell us that it has a tow somewhere astern and to navigate with caution until the tow can be clearly identified. The tow itself will be harder to spot, because it does not have white masthead lights, only the sidelights and sternlight. Even so, accidents have been very rare and who wants to tear off their keel or props on a large wire?

What can cause confusion is if large vessels are showing other lights which can be confused with the navigation lights. Rule 20(b) of the COLREGs expressly forbids this '… no other lights shall be exhibited, except such lights as cannot be mistaken for the lights specified in these Rules or do not impair their visibility…'

The only exception allowed to this is warships, which usually conform pretty closely to the rules, and working lights left on deck by fishermen. It is these working lights left on deck, despite the fact they are forbidden, which can confuse us, particularly on large vessels.

At the end of the day we are responsible for the safety of our own vessel and for avoiding worry and potential damage to others. The existing rules are clear and simple. Positioning of the lights, their colours, arcs and ranges are set down to avoid mistakes, sound signals are there to clarify what is around in fog.

These are facts that affect us every time we go to sea and a read through the rules from time to time is good investment in effort to prolong your life expectancy.

KEEPING A LOOKOUT

Even with the regulatory framework of the COLREGs there's no substitute for a sharp lookout.

How many times have we heard someone say after a collision that it was not their fault as they were on starboard and the other vessel was on port? Wrong. If a collision occurs both vessels are to blame. Read Rule 17 of the COLREGs.

Regulations for preventing collision at sea were introduced throughout the 19th century as sailing vessels got faster, governments talked to each other and steamers appeared. They were adopted internationally in 1897. These are the rules that still govern all vessels navigating on open seas and, with the exception of some local byelaws, in approaches to ports and inland waters.

Although the rules have been modified as situations have changed, they are logical, sensible and, above all, universally accepted. They take precedence over all other rules. To cope with the exceptional demands created by sailing boats racing closely, the racing rules cover issues such as overtaking and rounding of marks, but even these do not differ from the COLREGs in any material way.

But do yachtsmen really follow the COLREGs? How many are aware of the requirement to have a whistle or siren, for example? Annex 3 gives detailed specifications as to the volume and tone of the 'whistle' – the longer the vessel, the deeper the tone. Basically, for vessels of less than 20m in length, the audible range must be at least half a nautical mile (900m), or one mile for larger sailboats. For vessels under 12m, the whistle must be mounted as high as practical; on the mast above the sails maybe.

But why is a whistle important? The COLREGs state clearly that, under Rule 17, when the stand-on vessel thinks the give-way vessel is taking insufficient action, she shall indicate that doubt by five short blasts on the whistle and take action to best avoid a collision. Rule 34 adds that when power vessels are approaching each other, if the stand-on vessel decides to alter course to avoid a collision, she shall indicate the alteration with one short blast if altering to starboard, two short blasts if altering to port and three if the engines are put astern. Power yacht skippers take note: those of sailing yachts note that it does not apply to them.

How many yachtsmen have ever heard or sounded these signals? How many even have the whistle? Most yachts carry nothing more than a small aerosol-type foghorn, which is fine for a vessel of less than 12m but not for larger yachts.

One might say that collisions are comparatively rare, so why is this necessary? One answer is that yachts have become a lot faster in recent years; indeed many can compete with power yachts for speed. Consider two large racing yachts of, say, 60ft, reaching towards each other. Their closing speed could easily be 25 knots, or 14m a second.

If they recognise the danger at 100m apart, they have just 7.5 seconds to take action before they collide. In that time, how are skippers to indicate the action that the giving-way vessel is going to take to avoid misunderstandings? Would five short rapid blasts be heard if the boats are pounding along and the wind is carrying the sound to leeward? Would a hail of 'Starboard!' be heard at that distance on a windy day?

It might – just. But even if so, 7.5 seconds is very little time to assess the situation and take avoiding action. In addition, some modern sails do not allow a lookout beneath or around them and can block a sound signal. The only way to have a proper warning is from a lookout in the bow who is fully aware of the rules and has the confidence of the helmsman.

There are problems with the sound-signal regulation, of course. Can you imagine the chaos (not to mention the cacophony) if every boat started to sound five short blasts every time she was unsure of another boat's intentions during an event like the Round the Island race?

That event is exceptional because every boat keeps a proper lookout during the race for pure self-preservation. However, in a less crowded event or in an ocean race would the lookout be so keen?

NOT OVER-RELYING ON AIS

So crowded are harbours like the Solent, so popular is AIS, that ships' pilots admit they do not monitor Class B signals. Instead, it is up to yachtsmen to keep an ear on VTS, keep a sharp lookout and keep clear.

On a recent visit to the Vessel Tracking Service (VTS) tower in Southampton, I struck up a conversation with one of the pilots about the difficulties that he faced when bringing a vessel through the channel while approaching the port.

Of course, I wanted to know to what extent yachts were a problem in the narrow dredged channel and it was good to learn that, on the whole, yachts seemed to try to keep clear.

However, there is always the one sailor who does not see the approaching vessel or fails to appreciate how close he is getting, and for a pilot that one rogue sailor is a serious cause for concern.

The sight of a yacht sailing under the bows of a tanker off Cowes often prompts a comment from the uninitiated that power gives way to sail. There are two reasons why this is not the case. The first is the sheer impracticality of manoeuvring a large tanker in the narrow channel to Southampton, particularly as it approaches the big turn to the west of the Brambles Bank.

And a large turning vessel that tries to avoid a yacht in its path is very likely to lose control here. At this point the channel is narrow and the tides can be strong, so there is a high risk of the vessel going aground, and the last thing anyone wants is a large laden tanker grounding in the Solent, with all the attendant risks of an oil spill.

The second reason why large power does not give way is legal. The Southampton Port byelaws take precedence over the COLREGs within the limits of Southampton Port. Under these laws, a prohibition zone exists 1,000m in front of any vessel that is entering or leaving the port and for 100m on either side, and all vessels are required to keep out of this zone.

The limit is usually quite clear because a patrol craft will be stationed approximately 1,000m ahead of the vessel to try to clear other craft out of the way. So, the message is quite clear: keep a good lookout for commercial vessels approaching or leaving the port and ensure that you do not get within 1km of its bow or 100m of it on either side. Fail to adhere to this and it makes no difference if you are sailing, rowing or motoring – the outcome could well be a prosecution regardless of whether any damage was actually caused.

If the VHF has dual watch, it is worth keeping one channel on the VTS frequency as you approach any port just to keep up to date with the current information about shipping movements. Southampton was a commercial port long before yachts arrived on the scene. Today's harbour masters try to balance the port's current use and do their best to organise ship movements to avoid upsetting yachtsmen. But they are governed by the tides, so can only do so much.

In the course of our conversation, I asked the pilots to what extent AIS was of use to them. The answer, it turns out, is not very much at all as far as Class B sets are concerned. The reason is that there are now so many yachts in the Solent carrying AIS that Class B signals completely clutter up the screen if they are monitored.

It's hardly a surprise that pilots don't bother. They already have enough threats to their vessel to consider without such extra clutter and the byelaws give them the right of way in any case.

Within the Solent, therefore, you can be pretty certain that no commercial vessels will be picking up your AIS signal. Bear in mind, too, that the Class B system updates at 30 second intervals and during that time a yacht could tack or alter course.

Where AIS does come into its own, however, is in less crowded waters than those of the Solent – here, Class B is likely to be monitored. It is also a worthwhile addition in bad radar conditions such as in rough seas or in heavy rain, which can obliterate a small yacht on a radar screen.

So the advice from the professional pilots is that within the Solent – and I would expect that other commercial ports will operate similar policies – listen to VTS, keep a sharp lookout for shipping movements and keep out of the way. By all means switch on AIS, but do not rely upon its being watched by the large vessels that pose the greatest threat to yourself.

USING RADAR ALARMS

Thank heavens for radar alarms! Three close calls during the circumnavigation suggest many watch keepers are ignorant of – or just don't care about – the plight of yachts.

My recent circumnavigation has alerted me once again to the dangers of shipping when crossing oceans. Commercial ships give no indication of having seen a yacht, seldom if ever answer the VHF and very rarely alter course.

Most watch keepers have little idea about sailing, so have no understanding of what is involved in a course alteration by a yacht to give a greater clearance from them. It's not so bad when we are close-hauled, but when we have a spinnaker or a reacher set, it takes some time to get it down so the yacht can be manoeuvred.

I had three close calls on this last voyage. One vessel came from starboard on a collision course and I bore away to go under his stern. Another was overtaking on a closing course and I had to harden up to almost tack to give him clearance. The last ship was head to head and I bore away hard to show him my alteration, but I am not sure he had even noticed me.

I don't think that I missed any vessels. If I did it was because their radar was not on, so my Active Echo, a combined radar alarm and transponder, could not alert me. This piece of kit is an absolute must for ocean voyages because it sets off an alarm each time it receives a radar signal and returns an echo which should show on the other vessel's radar. It was pretty useless in sea areas whose shipping lanes receive heavy traffic such as the Channel because it would go off all the time. Nevertheless, the moment the alarm sounded I would go on deck and look around the horizon. If I could not see anything immediately I would switch on my own radar to try to find the target.

Obviously, the system's performance varies according to the weather conditions. In calm conditions I would normally receive the signal before anything appeared over the horizon, remembering that the radar horizon is 17 per cent greater than the visual one. But in rough weather the other vessel might be as close as two miles before the alarm went off, which gives little time to react. Fortunately, without exception, I only had jibs and mains set in rough weather, so was able to manoeuvre easily.

My radar could be set with safety zones, whereby an alarm sounded if a target appeared within a chosen box. I tended to use this close to the coasts and rely on the Active Echo out at sea.

I do not know why ships' crews should appear to be so casual about altering course for a yacht. Far more yachts now cross oceans than ever before, so they must be a fairly common sight. One can appreciate the imperative to make a fast passage to keep to a schedule, but a few degrees for a few minutes will hardly affect this.

There is an attitude that the merchant ship is working for a living while the yachtsmen is just having a good time, but we don't see heavy goods vehicles deliberately carving up cars. The COLREGs are quite clear and make no mention of large ships being able to flout them if the other vessel is a yacht, except in confined waters where separate byelaws apply, such as in the Solent. In addition, the watch keepers are likely to be far more experienced than the average yachtsman, which is an even better reason for them to be alert.

I was especially puzzled by a number of vessels I saw that did not have their radars on in mid-ocean. This is fine if the watch keeper is keeping a visual lookout, but many don't. And the radar reflector carried aboard nearly every yacht, which gives some warning of its presence, is only useful so long as the other vessel's radar is turned on. If anything caused me sustained stress on this voyage, it was this worry about shipping. The constant need to be alert, keeping a lookout with whatever means at one's disposal and at the back of your mind the thought that there might be a ship creeping up unobserved and unobserving is something I can do without.

When sailing single-handed, I cannot keep a visual lookout all the time and I accept the risk from that, but I now find that the worry is removing my enjoyment of the solitude at sea. In truth, I don't think I shall make another long oceanic solo voyage again – I want the comfort of a 24-hour visual lookout in future.

THROWING A HEAVING LINE

It seems few yachtsmen are adept at the under-rated skill of throwing a heaving line nowadays, yet a well-hurled line can save the blushes of both skipper and crew alike.

Judging from examples I have witnessed recently, the art of throwing a heaving line (or any line come to that) is in danger of being forgotten. All too often you see a line thrown from a boat that fails to reach the intended recipient, although there was plenty of line to cover the distance. When you see the line tangle within a metre of the thrower's arm you know the line was not prepared properly.

This is not just frustrating, it is embarrassing to the thrower. Worse, the failure to get a line ashore might force a boat to make another approach or could cause difficulties if a strong wind is blowing the bows off a pontoon or wharf. And although a heaving line is just a messenger to increase the range you can send a line, it becomes essential when you are trying to transfer a towline or painter to or from another boat or a liferaft.

The secret of getting a heaving line safely to its intended destination is having the right heaving line to start with and preparing to throw it properly. Any rope can be thrown and be made to cover quite a distance if it is prepared and thrown correctly, but a proper heaving line will enable contact to be made at a greater distance. The secret to throwing a line is to ensure the line is clear to run and the impetus is given to the throwing end of the line in the right direction.

A simple method is to start at the non-throwing end and just flake it on to the deck until you come to the end you want to throw, then start making a small coil, perhaps four or five turns with a diameter of no more than 0.5m. Now make another coil of the same size about 1m behind the first one. Smaller coils mean the line is less likely to tangle and easier to throw.

Make sure the inner end of the line is made fast to something, perhaps a heavier line that is to be sent across, but anything secure like a stanchion will do – you look pretty stupid if you throw a heaving line and the whole lot goes out! Then pick up the two coils, one in each hand, make sure they are lying clear and not tangled and that you have good swinging room. Try your swing first to make sure it is comfortable, then swing back and hurl the line. The outer end is aimed at the destination and the inner coil is flung out as well so that the line has the least possible drag.

To throw a line effectively is a matter of preparation and practice. It is one of those things you can practise when stormbound and is a very useful skill to add to your armoury. Like every aspect of sailing, the chances of things going wrong increase proportionally to the reduction in time available to prepare, so if you think you are going to need to use a heaving line or just throw a mooring line ashore, prepare it in plenty of time.

If you do not have a heaving line, they are quite easy to make. You need about 28m of light line, about 8mm in diameter. Now comes the fun bit – making a monkey's fist in the end. I won't attempt to describe it, but find a book, which shows you how to do it. Get it good and tight, so it becomes a small dense ball. We used to put a large metal nut inside them, but a golf ball is pretty good. This helps to make the end heavier and will greatly extend the distance you will be able to throw it.

One other method of throwing a messenger is to use a Bolas, a light line with a heavy weight at the end copied from the gauchos of South America. You swing it around your head with about 3m from hand to weight, then try and let it go so that the weight travels in the desired direction. That you need more swinging space than is normally available on a yacht is one problem. But a bigger one is that I have never seen the weight travel where it was wanted – in fact it was more of a danger to people close by on deck.

THE ART OF ANCHORING

The best techniques for anchoring don't include dropping all the chain right on top of the anchor, as I saw done recently.

Watching a yacht drop her anchor and then allow a large quantity of chain to drop straight down on top of it was a reminder that not everyone has picked up the safest techniques.

With modern anchors like the CQR and Danforth, which have no stock and do not leave any part sticking up above the bottom, dropping all the anchor cable on the anchor is no longer so risky as it was. But if the anchor had been a fisherman type, the chain could have caught around the exposed fluke and dragged it out, as the weight would have been coming on the wrong part of the anchor and prevented it from digging in.

Whichever you use, it is best to drop back once the anchor is on the bottom, and pay out the chain as you go. That way the anchor tends to be tugged into the bottom more effectively.

You can soon tell whether or not the anchor is holding: put your hand on the cable and if it is jumping or vibrating, it has probably not dug in. The only way to deal with this is to pay out more cable. Of course, some bottoms are very hard to dig into. Hard gravel, such as is found in parts of the Thames, is one example – the anchor may never hold unless there is enough weight in it. Even then I doubt anyone would sleep comfortably knowing that a brief squall could send the boat drifting if it depended only on the weight of the anchor and cable.

So the basic idea is to drop the anchor onto the bottom – and you can usually tell when it reaches the seabed because the weight on the cable lessens, or the cable may start to oscillate instead of running straight down – then pay out a minimum of three times the maximum depth at high water.

That would apply to a sheltered anchorage. In more exposed anchorages you will want to pay out more. Even if the anchor is holding well, it can become vulnerable when the tide or wind changes and the boat swings round. The anchor will come free as the pull arrives from a different direction, and you want the anchor to dig in as quickly as possible. Anchors usually cope with this perfectly well, but you may lose a few feet on the bottom as it digs itself in again in the new direction. This is when the pull needs to be horizontal. The cautious sailor would set their alarm for this moment just to ensure that the anchor has dug in again properly.

What you are trying to ensure is that the cable at the anchor is always pulling horizontally and not leading straight up. This is one of the reasons why, even if you use rope for the anchor cable, there should always be a length of chain attached to the anchor first. The other reason is that rope can snag on objects on the bottom and get cut or worn whereas chain will usually cause more harm to the obstruction than to itself.

The usual suggestion is a minimum of ten metres of chain on any anchor, but if you are going cruising round the world, frankly you would be better off with all chain. We lost an anchor in a Greenland fjord even though it was on a very heavy line because it snapped in a particularly ferocious, hurricane-strength squall.

With anchors, weight does matter. There are tables that show the holding capabilities of various sizes and types of anchor, and there have been some clever developments in recent years that have led to lighter anchors with greater holding power. They do work, on the right sea bottom, but a weightier anchor of good design will always perform better than a lighter one to the same design.

But don't think that a heavier anchor means you can use lighter chain. The chain still has to be strong enough to hold the weight of the boat against a strong tidal stream coupled with a heavy squall, and that means it must pull out horizontally. For some years I have had five fathoms of chain larger than that recommended attached to the anchor – a CQR – just to help ensure that the rode is going to do just that.

UNSNAGGING AN ANCHOR

Your anchor has snagged on an obstruction and you don't want to lose it. What do you do? Brute force, strategic motoring or a helpful neighbour should do the trick.

There are a few things more frustrating than trying to weigh anchor and discovering that your anchor has snagged on some obstruction on the seabed. The first thing to do is check the chart and make sure you have not snagged a power cable. If you have, then you have lost your anchor and, apart from the danger to those aboard if the power cable is damaged, you won't be popular with the people who suddenly find themselves deprived of the benefits of modern living that electricity supplies.

If the chart shows no obstruction, then you can confidently start to extricate the anchor. The problem is likely to be a wire chain and providing it is not too heavy you may well get yourself clear. A wreck can be more difficult as there may be other obstructions.

If your anchor cable is all line, with no chain, it could cut through pretty quick in which case saving a little money by not buying yourself 10m of chain is going to cost you an anchor.

Assuming that you have chain on your anchor cable, the easiest and most expensive solution is to slip the anchor cable. Put a buoy on the end, though, if you have not automatically buoyed the anchor – which is not common these days – as you might be able to find a diver to try to extricate the anchor at a later date. But don't leave it there too long as local divers know the value of anchor and chain and you might return and find your buoy and anchor has disappeared and it already being offered second hand at a local boat jumble.

A better solution is to apply as much lifting power as you can and, if that fails to shift it, try motoring or sailing in the opposite direction to that in which you were lying and see whether you can draw the anchor out that way. It is best to do this in astern as you will pretty stupid if you catch the line around the propeller.

If you have anchored in hard clay, it well could be that the anchor has ploughed into the seabed and become jammed – force will get it clear. However, after anchoring in hard clay-like sand for two weeks on a Danforth anchor, we found the flukes broke off when we applied tension.

Failing this, more brute force can be applied by tying off the anchor cable and allowing a rising tide to do the lifting for you. If the bow starts to go down too much, ease out again and try something else. Sometimes it is possible to lift the anchor and its obstruction to the surface, or at least close enough so it can be reached from the boat, a dinghy, or by a crew swimming.

Put a line around the obstruction with both ends aboard, one end secured so it can be slipped from the cleat, bollard or by a round turn and two half hitches, a knot that can be let go under strain. Then ease out on the anchor cable. It should drop free of the obstruction and can now be hauled aboard. Then let go of your line from the cleat, etc., and then the obstruction will fall free to the bottom.

If this fails, then slide a small loop of chain on the end of a line down the anchor cable. Your objective is to get this chain to the point where you think the anchor cable is shackled to the shank of the anchor, so keeping the anchor cable taut helps. The weight of the chain will allow it to drop. If there is another boat about, ask them to take the line on your rescue chain and head away from you in the direction you think the anchor is lying.

The objective is to get the chain beneath the shank and right up to the crown of the anchor. Then you can ease out your own chain and your anchor will be drawn out from under whatever is holding it and break free.

CLEARING THE PROPELLER

Each year the RNLI answers 250 Mayday or Pan calls from the yachts with something round the prop. Many surely did not merit a call for help.

Why are so many sailors frightened of the water? It's as if beneath the surface of the sea lurk unimaginable dangers and monsters waiting to trip those who enter. Each year the RNLI answer 250 Mayday or Pan calls from yachts with something tangled around their prop. Yet it is often fairly simple to dive down and clear the obstruction.

The average cost of launching a lifeboat, around £6,000, is a heavy price for an institution that relies on voluntary contributions. Leaving aside that a Mayday should only be used for a life-threatening emergency, such as sinking, a fire or explosion, or a Pan call is to indicate urgency but no immediate threat to life, the problem is that people panic before they stop to think whether they can help themselves.

The degree of emergency usually comes down to the situation of the yacht. If it were motoring towards a rocky lee shore and could not set sails, there might be some urgency to obtain assistance before the yacht ran ashore (unless it could anchor safely). But if the wind were offshore and would blow the yacht clear of danger, or sails set to clear the coast, there is no need for any call for assistance at all. Get back out to sea and sort out the problem.

We have grown so used to calling someone to assist when anything goes wrong – in part because modern cars and household machinery are so complicated that repairs are beyond the ability of most of us – that we all call for assistance instinctively when anything goes wrong.

So if an engine fails we call in an expert. But we can't call out an engineer when we are at sea so, instead of stopping to think how the problem could be resolved, we call the coastguard.

We need to rethink this. Before engines became reliable and failures were frequent, people coped without screaming for help all the time.

The coastguards received 77 calls during this year's Round the Island Race. How many were really serious? It was difficult to prioritise them and there are just not enough lifeboat stations around to answer every call immediately.

But back to entangled propellers. Whatever happened to jumping overside with a knife or hacksaw to cut the rope free? Most yachts have their props within an easy reach of the surface. All that is required is a pair of goggles and a cutting instrument. A wet or dry suit would be convenient in colder waters. If a scuba equipment is carried, so much better.

The only change between now and 50 to 100 years ago is that the modern boats tend to have higher freeboards, so getting back on board again can be difficult. But don't many boats have a swimming ladder of some sort? How many times has an owner looked at his or her boat and thought about how to climb back on board, unaided if necessary? If they haven't, they should do it now.

It can be argued that jumping into the water to clear an obstruction is less risky than climbing the mast at sea. Yet we often climb the masts in port or when we have a problem. We don't think anything of it – we just accept it as something that happens and we get on with it. So why don't we have the same attitude towards going into the water?

I have met people who have no fear of a swimming pool, but are terrified of going in the water whilst out at sea. The film *Jaws* is partly to blame for this, but sharks usually take a while to realise anyone is in the water and come to investigate, if they are around at all.

So next time you are in a sheltered anchorage, put over a ladder and dive in (without a lifejacket as you cannot get underwater wearing one) then put on goggles and check the propeller. Holding your breath underwater is not as difficult as it seems. There is a wonderful world to explore beneath the surface of the sea, apart from the chance to check the hull below the waterline without recourse to boat hoists or divers.

MANOEUVRING INTO A BERTH

Combine the forces of tide and wind, factor in prop-walk, now throw in limited space and it's little wonder that many able skippers quail at the thought of mooring manoeuvres.

Manoeuvring any boat effectively is a combination of understanding the characteristics of the vessel, allowing for the wind force and for any tidal effects. First, be sure to find out what sort of propeller there is in a single-screw boat; that means does it turn clockwise or anti-clockwise when going ahead? This has a fundamental effect on how the boat will manoeuvre under power.

A clockwise direction going forward will produce a tendency for the bow to slew slightly to port when going ahead. But the reverse effect, which pulls the stern into a berth, is more pronounced because most propellers are designed to be more efficient going ahead, so the paddlewheel effect, or transverse thrust, is greater when going astern.

The way to work out this paddlewheel effect is to take the movement of the propeller below its boss, as the propeller has more grip the further it is below the surface.

It is when trying to berth in a crowded river with a strong tide that the skills required are put to the test. "Time spent on reconnaissance is seldom time wasted," the Duke of Wellington said, and this is especially true when berthing in difficult circumstances or a strange port. The chart or almanac should be examined before making an entrance and, if there is any doubt, approach slowly with an eye on the echo sounder.

With a berth chosen you have another decision to make – how best to approach it and make fast.

Always try to berth against the tide if there is an option. It is usual to come in alongside and put out the head and stern lines first. If only the forward back spring has been put ashore, once it has been made fast the boat can motor against it and sheer into the pontoon if necessary.

Don't try putting out the aft spring first when coming in against the tide as the rudder may have to be used to keep the bow from yawing off the pontoon – if that starts it is best to let go and go round and try again. To avoid this situation, get the bow line ashore first. If you have to come in with the tide it pays to put out the stern line and the forward spring first.

Leaving a berth, springs can be very effective. If there is no tide let go everything except the forward back spring, place a good fender near the bow between the boat and the berth, put the helm over so the rudder is turning the bow into the berth and motor gently forward.

The stern will swing out clear of the berth until it is possible to put the rudder over the other way, go slow astern and let go the spring. When the tide is against you, all lines can be let go except the aft spring, whereupon the rudder is put over away from the pontoon, so that the bow will sheer clear.

If the tide is coming from astern, then holding onto the bow spring and judicious use of rudder will cant the stern out and enable the boat to back out. The springs are particularly useful if there are other boats moored close ahead and astern.

One of the best exponents of the use of springs was one Derek 'Spiro' Ling, a Thames barge skipper who started work afloat at the age of 14. Racing in barge matches with him was a joy, but the real pleasure was to watch him manoeuvre a large barge with limited horsepower in very limited space among barges on the Thames. Often the whole operation of berthing was achieved with no fuss using just one spring.

Like everything in life, there is an enormous pleasure in watching a true professional go about their work. There's even more when you are a part of it, if only a small part.

As with nearly all elements of boat handling, these manoeuvres are best practised a few times in calm conditions, so you can gain experience in handling the boat and build up confidence.

It's also important to let other members of the crew practise as well, not just so they can bring the boat in if you are injured, but because it boosts their confidence. For a skipper, there are few things more satisfying than to watch someone you have taught complete a manoeuvre well.

TOWING TECHNIQUES

It might appear to be a simple act, but it's surprising how much people don't know about towing, yet getting it right can save a lot of aggravation down the line.

Watching a RIB trying to tow a large yacht reminded me of how little some people know about towing.

If you attach the tow line to the back of a tug which is smaller than the tow, then the tow is in charge. The tug cannot manoeuvre because its stern is firmly held. It can put on as many revolutions as it likes, but raw power is of no use if the stern is held and making you pull in the wrong direction. If you look at commercial tugs, there is a very good reason why the tow hook is near the centre of the vessel; it is because the tug can pivot when it has a load on its tow line and so move itself in any direction while towing.

The tow point on a RIB needs to be a good third of the length of the boat towards the bow from the stern if the RIB is to exercise any real control over its direction and be an effective tug.

The problem here is that many RIBs have an inverted 'U' mast across their sterns – and an outboard engine can snag the line as well. A tall towing post, to keep the tow line clear of these obstructions, is going to take a lot of supporting, apart from putting on a heeling moment which could be done without.

Using a bridle

One solution, which avoids a towing post, is to tow from a bridle. Both ends of a rope are made fast, one on each side of the tow boat, as close to amidships as possible. Then find the middle of the rope and put a half hitch in it. Attach the tow line to the loop of this half hitch.

This enables a tow boat to pivot and makes controlling the tow very much easier. It is important to watch that the bridle does not drop down and catch the propeller, especially when starting the tow. Once there is tension on the tow line, the bridle will usually be clear of the water.

The length of tow line will depend on the sea conditions and the manoeuvring space. If there is a big sea, a long tow line is required to avoid snatching – sudden jerks as the towline tightens – which can lead to a tow line parting or damage to securing points. Putting a weight in the middle of a long tow line, such as a rubber tyre, or a length of anchor chain, will act as a 'spring' and reduce or remove the snatching.

This is safe at sea, but when you close port the need to manoeuvre in a confined space means that a short tow line is needed. If very tight manoeuvring is needed, it is often better to attach the tug to the stern of the tow, but the best control in this situation is often exercised if the tug's stern overlaps the tow's stern.

A safe lead on the tow

One of the major points to ensure a safe tow is to find a good towing point on the tow itself and a safe lead at the bow. Look around the foredeck on most yachts and try to find a secure point – capable of taking the weight of the boat in theory – to which a tow line can be secured. How many mooring cleats would you trust to take the weight in a big seaway?

The tow line also needs to be led through something at the bow so its pull is focused there. Gammon plates these days seldom have a 'Panama' lead, but if the boat ever needs a tow it would have been better if they had.

What is a Panama lead? Fairleads are open at the top, but the height of the locks in the Panama Canal meant that mooring lines led upwards and would jump out of the top, so a 'closed' lead was introduced from which the mooring line could not jump free.

On some boats being towed, a bridle can be rigged from each shoulder of the boat, but this will mean the helm will have to be manned throughout the tow, whereas if the tow line passes through a lead at the bow, the helm can be left lashed amidships.

If a strong cleat is not fitted forward, the mast is often used to secure the line, but this can cause damage. It is better to take the line back to a sheet winch, ideally on a bridle, so the load is shared by winches on both sides, and tied off there.

SAILING SAFELY

It doesn't always pay to push on harder in bad
weather. The boat that is sailed safely is not only
the most comfortable; it is often the fastest too.

When do you decide to stop racing (or continuing on your desired
course) because of deteriorating weather conditions? Your attitude to this
issue will depend on where the boat is sailing and for how long. In a day-
race around the Solent, a boat can be over-pushed because the worst that
can happen is a wipe-out and repairs can be made that evening. One race
lost in a series can be recovered by good performances in the remainder.

But longer ocean races require a different approach. There are no
repair yards, sail or rigging lofts out at sea. All sail and rigging repairs
have to be undertaken on board, which diverts crew from concentrating
on the racing. A torn sail will slow a boat and a rigging failure can mean
retirement.

There comes a point in very bad weather at sea when conditions
deteriorate to such a point that there is a serious risk of damage if a boat
continues to be pushed. Its fabric and rigging come under threat and the
crew are likely to become frightened or exhausted, so less effective.

At this point pressing on becomes self-defeating or a dangerous
gamble. If damage is sustained, at best the boat's sailing performance is
reduced. At worst it may have to head to port for repairs. Either way, the
race is lost or the voyage hindered. If close to land, it may pay to find a
lee and even anchor, whereas out at sea (provided there is searoom, of
course) the right decision might be to heave to or at least snug the boat

down so that it rides the waves more easily.

The decision to delay the start of the Fastnet Race, so that boats would be close to shelter rather than exposed in the Irish Sea when the bad weather hit, was always the right one to my mind. Many of the competitors must have heaved a sigh of relief as they entered a sheltered port. A racing purist might find this anathema, almost as if their masculinity is under threat unless they are perceived to be gung-ho. But you only have to look at the number of boats that pull out of races with damage when conditions get nasty to appreciate that the old adage applies: to finish 1st, first you have to finish.

Boasting about how tough you were looks pretty stupid if you had to pull out of a race because the boat pressed on when it should have eased up. It is tantamount to boasting about poor seamanship.

When racing, I have told the crew to stop pushing and make the boat comfortable on a number of occasions. Slowing down, so the boat does not slam and rides as easily as possible in the waves, may seem pusillanimous, but it reduces the risk of damage. It also takes some of the pressure off the crew and allows them to relax a bit. A few miles may be lost, but they can be recovered quickly once the wind and waves ease because everything aboard the boat is still working and the crew are fresher and not having to devote their energies to repairing any damage incurred.

The time that is lost in repairing a sail that should be set for the conditions means speed is lost and even one knot adds up quickly. Indeed, it can be the margin that separates winning from losing even in a short ocean race. Repairs also tire the crew. Rather than racing, they have to work long hours to repair a sail as quickly as possible. And if position reports are being received, the slow slipping of position and distance is damaging for morale.

The same attitude applies when reducing sail in bad weather. It often pays to bear off downwind to allow the crew to work more safely and more effectively on the foredeck. This will also reduce the apparent wind, which means the sails will thrash around less. Of course, a few hundred yards distance might be lost to leeward, but compare that with the extra time that is lost because the crew have to fight a flogging sail on a wave-washed foredeck, not to mention the potential for damage to the sail itself.

COPING WITH BIG SEAS & HIGH WINDS

Big seas and high winds have always been a fact of sailors' lives. What has changed is the comparative inexperience of those seeking to make long passages, who find themselves in a situation beyond their capabilities.

I suspect that I am not alone, when hearing of the rescue of another yacht's crew, in thinking: 'There but for the grace of God go I.' Those of us who go to sea regularly know that it can become dangerous very quickly and create circumstances that will threaten the best found and prepared yacht and crew and so we superstitiously hesitate to criticise others.

Every rescue is a reflection on our sport, adding to the statistics used by those who wish to introduce more controls. We are all affected, whether we like it or not, which is why those unprepared should think twice before setting out on ambitious voyages that may be beyond their capabilities.

In August there were two rescues in the Bay of Biscay within days of each other which emphasise the dangers of being caught out by rough weather. In one incident, the yacht, far from new, lost her rudder and the crew were taken off by helicopter.

In the other, the crew were suffering from seasickness and found after three days that they could cope no longer. The Royal Navy pulled them to safety in conditions that were described as 'horrendous' – Force 9 with 30ft waves.

The use of the word 'horrendous' worries me as it gives the impression that circumstances were unusual. Thirty-foot high waves are not uncommon out in the oceans, neither is a Force 9 wind; they are very uncomfortable, but not abnormal.

Horrendous, in the circumstances, describes this particular crew's reaction to the conditions, because that is how they appeared to them. It was obviously beyond their capabilities, but would not have seemed so bad to a professional seafarer or experienced yachtsman.

The trouble is that exaggerations like this tend to be used as an excuse for the failure of the boat and crew, but everyone who goes to sea has to accept that they are entering the big boys' world. They cannot expect lesser conditions because of their lack of experience, nor claim that the circumstances were overwhelming because they could not cope with them.

The oceanic conditions will be those that Nature decides to produce and they have been the same for centuries. What has changed is the comparative inexperience and naïveté of some of those seeking to make long voyages. Of course, they do not go to sea seeking adverse weather, but if we start to cross oceans and spend long enough at sea, the law of averages says we shall run into rough weather from time to time.

Even the mighty QE2 found herself almost hove to in mid-Atlantic when she ran into hurricane Luis in September 1995. Then she was struck by a wave estimated to be 28m in height which swamped the whole foredeck, including the bridge. (She had already lost her port navigation light, 27m above the sea, to another wave!) It was a rogue wave, described as looking like the white cliffs of Dover as it advanced, and outside the experience of the officers on board.

Such rogues do occur – infrequently, thank goodness, as few yachts would survive anything that ferocious. Sailors have a duty to consider how they might cope with such conditions or delay setting out on a long voyage until they are truly ready.

The fact is that neither yacht should have been at sea in the situation they found themselves in last August when they nearly lost their lives.

It is the real world out at sea. There is no escape, no 'Beam me up, Scotty' or switching channels when things get nasty. In most cases the crews find themselves unexpectedly alone and frightened, dependent upon their own resources which may not be adequate for the test in a life and death struggle.

They won't always find themselves within range of a lifeboat or a conveniently nearby Royal Navy carrier whose crews will risk their futures to provide the unwary with a second chance of life.

TESTING MOB PROCEDURES

The report into the death of a skipper while tethered to his yacht inspired me to conduct some trials of my own. My findings were alarming.

I have never fallen overside while attached by a safety line, but I had always assumed I would be recovered easily if I was held to the boat. The death of Christopher Reddish while sailing Reflex 38 *Lion* in a RORC Cowes-Cherbourg Fastnet qualifier last June showed this is not necessarily the case. But how and why had the sailor drowned? Yachtsmen analyse disasters to learn from them, so I sailed into the Solent with a dummy that weighed 65kg when full of water, fitted it with a lifejacket and attached it to the safety jackstay on deck with a tether.

In our first experiment, the dummy was thrown over from the foredeck, the area from which Reddish is thought to have slipped. Even while sailing at just four knots, the dummy floated face-down as it dragged through the water. This was not at all what we expected and would have quickly drowned a real casualty.

When we slowed, the dummy turned face up, but it bashed against the side with sufficient force to cause head injuries. Heaving the dummy on board required two strong crew, but at least it pulled the head clear of the water. Even more alarming was what happened when the dummy went over from the cockpit. It was swept aft into the wake alongside the transom and had to be hauled forward before recovery could be attempted. Again, this had not been anticipated.

Of course, the tether length had a considerable effect. If it was too long, the body fell well into the sea, but if it was too short, working on deck was difficult. Either way, you were vulnerable if the tether was clipped on in the wrong position. Our conclusion was clear: fasten a tether to the high side of the boat or a hard point near the centreline with a tether that would not allow you to be completely immersed.

The other thing we learnt was that to recover someone quickly, before they risk drowning while being towed, you should stop the boat immediately. If sailing, luff up into the wind. This has the added benefit that if the casualty has fallen over the lee side (more likely than the windward side), the boat comes upright as it comes into the wind, so may lift the casualty clear of the water.

Much has been written about how to recover people in the water. At Clipper we carried a life-sling for this, but we found it hard to put around the dummy on our trials. Now we think a lifejacket should have a clear tag attached to its harness which can be connected quickly by a rope or a clip.

If the person cannot be hauled back on board by sheer muscle – and that depends on the strength of those on deck and the weight of the person in the water – we use a spinnaker halyard because if it is reeved through a crane, which it should be on ocean-going yachts, it can be led aft easily. With the halyard taken to a winch, there is more than sufficient power to heave even a heavy person back on board speedily.

Other points that came across in our trial were the importance of a clear roster of who was in charge if someone went over and good communication with the helm. I also found it informative to challenge my assumptions. Bodies in the water did not behave as we had expected and their recovery was far more difficult than anticipated. We had plenty of hands. The problems would be greater and recovery slower when shorthanded. It's fair to assume adrenalin would help when heaving a casualty inboard, but I wouldn't want to risk my life on it.

Every incident will be different and the important thing is to run through each beforehand. But the key points from our trial are: don't fall overside in the first place; be sure you are seen if you do; clip on to the high side of the deck or amidships with a tether that won't let you fall completely into the water; and always, stop the boat immediately.

Finally, don't assume what we learnt will necessarily work for you in every case. Go and try it for yourself.

DEALING WITH MEDICAL EMERGENCIES

When Clipper skippers sought medevacs to treat two serious injuries in the Southern Ocean in November, they did what all yachtsmen should do in the face of illness at sea – play it safe.

The Southern Ocean is having one of its windy years. In November, two people were injured during the Clipper Race. One on *Mission Performance* suffered a cleat arm penetrating his oilskins and spearing him in the lower leg; a nasty wound, not life-threatening in itself, but not one the skipper wanted to risk treating aboard. Another crew member onboard *Derry-Londonderry-Doire* fell heavily and bruised their arm so badly that the nurse aboard could not be certain or not if it was broken.

The boats headed towards Port Elizabeth, South Africa, where a lifeboat of the National Sea Rescue Institution took the injured ashore. Fortunately, the arm was not broken, but the skipper made the right call – better to be certain than risk permanent damage and infection.

It's not just the Southern Ocean which dishes out the heavy stuff. Eighteen months ago a Clipper boat was pooped in the Northern Pacific, an area that can be just as bad. Four crew were injured as the wave smashed over the stern and conditions were deemed too dangerous to try to make a recovery by helicopter from a US Coastguard cutter, so a RIB was used. This was successful and when conditions had improved and land was in range the helicopter took the injured people to hospital in California.

Injury or illness aboard a yacht on an oceanic voyage can be a nightmare for skippers. The gravity of a situation is only slightly reduced if the skipper happens to be a medical professional because even doctors face difficulties with the facilities on the average yacht. Armed solely with something like the *Ship Captain's Medical Guide*, it is very hard for the non-professional to be certain of the cause and extent of the problem.

Medical advice is available through the Coastguard's Maritime Rescue Co-ordination Centres (MRCCs) and there are organisations that specialise in supplying verbal assistance. But despite this back-up, the skipper is the man on the spot and has to deal with the actual problem.

The easiest problems are external, heavy bruising or bone fractures. It is much harder to identify an internal illness or damage. Uncertainty is what creates the concern and dilemmas about the best course of action. A broken limb can be strapped up, but how does someone know whether they have done it properly? Broken bones will start to knit quite quickly, but you don't want the patient to have to face a fracture being reset because it was not done properly the first time.

It is possible to hold some internal problems at bay through certain drugs, but how long do you keep that up? It is hardly surprising that most skippers when faced with these choices will look for somewhere close that has proper medical facilities, so as to transfer the casualty to capable hands as fast as possible. Vessels are sometimes around – the MRCCs will locate the nearest in an emergency – with a hospital and proper medicine chest. But it is unlikely that a cargo vessel has a doctor; just crew who have probably done the same first aid training as the yacht skipper.

Small surprise, then, that when most skippers face a serious injury or illness they will request a medevac. A cargo ship is the most likely immediate source because it will be heading for a port and faster than the yacht. Closer to land a helicopter can take a person off and sometimes within range and to save time, a lifeboat or harbour launch can rendezvous, although transfers between boats at sea can be their own hazard.

We all hope to cross an ocean without medical problems, but it makes sense to be prepared for the worst; if nothing else, if one is prepared, Murphy's Law says nothing will happen. Keep a medical book like the *Ship Captain's Medical Guide* on board and ensure that the medical kit is equipped to deal with emergencies and the drugs to hold an illness or infection at bay until land is reached. Finally, make sure you know how to make contact for medical advice and have the communication equipment to do so. Lives are too precious to be risked by a lack of easy precautions.

TRANSFERRING CREW MEMBERS

When you have to transfer crew from one boat to another in mid-ocean, the accepted method is not always the best, as the Clipper fleet found out.

The accepted method of transferring someone from one boat to another at sea by means of a liferaft may not be the right answer in some conditions.

In the current Clipper round the world race, one crew member seriously injured his leg when the boat was careering downwind in gusts of up to 30 knots of wind and 15ft waves. A tourniquet was immediately applied to staunch the flow of blood, but it was obvious that, if the foot was to be saved, a person with medical experience was urgently needed aboard.

Fortunately a competing yacht had a recently retired surgeon in its crew and was only 26 miles away. It responded immediately to the PAN call and arrived on the scene three hours later.

The seas were heavy so there was no question of the two yachts going alongside each other as this would have caused serious damage and probably injured more crew, so there were two alternative methods of effecting a transfer. One was to let the doctor swim across, wearing a lifejacket and harness with a safety line attached; the second was to use a liferaft.

The water was warm, about 25°C, but the decision was taken to go by the book, launch a liferaft with the doctor in it and then either tow this astern or throw a line so the other boat could come alongside and pick up the passenger.

The eight-person liferaft was launched with some difficulty and inflated. Unfortunately, it inflated upside down and it took some time in the large seas to get it righted. The doctor boarded with difficulty and the painter was eased to allow the raft to float clear. At this point the raft's sea anchor brought up, but as the raft and yacht moved, this sea anchor caught around the skeg.

Trying to pull it clear resulted in the painter breaking – they are meant to break under a certain strain, of course, so that when abandoning a yacht the liferaft does not get dragged down when the yacht sinks.

The doctor was now in the liferaft and in danger of being crushed as the stern rose and fell in the swell so he was brought back on board. Efforts to attach another line to the raft proved fruitless. This method was now abandoned.

The priority was to get the doctor to the patient, so the raft was left caught under the counter and a line thrown to the other boat, which came close in alongside for the purpose. This line was led to a block amidships on the receiving boat, where there was the least danger to the doctor of being crushed and freeboard was at its minimum. The line was attached to the doctor's harness and a retaining line secured just in case. The doctor then jumped into the sea and was hauled across the narrow gap and lifted aboard in less than half a minute.

The liferaft was proving extremely difficult to disentangle from the skeg. Now half full of water, the raft had no point to attach any line to, to heave it aboard and it was too heavy to be lifted by its canopy.

Since it could not be recovered nor left floating around in case it started a search and rescue alert, it was slashed to deflate and the bits hauled back on board.

In this incident the liferaft proved to be a distraction. The doctor could have been transferred quite quickly, probably within ten minutes if the lifejacket, harness and line method had been used from the start. Instead, almost an hour was wasted.

The view of those involved was that it would be better not to bother with the raft if this happened again and just use the line system. Even in cold water the doctor would be in the water for such a short time he would not have time to get really cold.

GEAR

"There's something illogical about carrying highly expensive equipment and not knowing something as fundamental as its capabilities, limitations and what it really looks like."

Robin Knox-Johnston, May 1997

SOLENT SYNDROME

A plea to the yachting industry: engineer for the
real-world conditions we sailors experience, not
the averages your theories might suggest.

22 years ago I was sheltering with my wife and daughter aboard *Suhaili*
in Ramsgate, trying to get west. The weather was not encouraging and to
avoid an unpleasant bash to windward we stayed alongside. It seemed a
chance to practise some techniques, so I trained the crew how to throw
a heaving line. Dick Johnson, editor of *Yachting World*, was sheltering
for the same reason and having watched us for a while, came aboard and
suggested I write a column for his magazine. That is how this page started.

The world of yachting has seen some interesting developments while
I have been writing this column. Designs have improved, materials have
changed and equipment has made great strides. Attitudes and techniques
have adapted as well, and the way I learned to navigate and sail no longer
seem so appropriate to the modern generation of yachtsmen. Just two
examples will suffice: we no longer need to understand astro-navigation
and I doubt many yachtsmen today could splice a wire.

While these inventions have simplified sailors' lives and made them
safer, other developments have been less desirable, particularly the one I
call the Solent Syndrome. This is the attitude of engineers, designers and
manufacturers to design boats suitable for day or weekend sailing around
the Solent and to overlook what happens on longer voyages.

Part of the problem is the reliance on theory and the lack of ocean-
going experience. Remember how recently scientists discovered what

sailors had known for years, that waves of 30m or more do exist? Similarly, theory fails to take account of the fact that the loadings created by a gale in a large seaway or the sudden snatch-loads in a knockdown or when a small violent cyclone suddenly reverses the wind direction are far greater than the theoretical static loads.

In the Solent or close to a coast, a breakage can be fixed during the week when the boat is in the marina, so the effect is minimal. Loose leeward rigging may be fine when you can change it and the worst is a short motor back to port if the mast breaks. But shaking rigging hardens and will fail far more quickly – and you don't want to jury rig in mid-ocean.

Chain plates, goosenecks, sail tracks and deck eyebolts all need to be strong enough to take shock loadings. Eric Hiscock always recommended that chain plates should extend for five hull strakes, a system we adopted when we built *Suhaili*. That was based on a great deal of ocean-crossing experience.

Another example is that bearings (such as on rudders) that might be adequate for the calm waters of the Solent may not be strong enough for the forces that come with larger wave movements. When there are twin rudders, the slapping effect of the weather rudder hitting waves when out of the water can put huge loads on bearings, something which does not seem to be considered when calculations are made.

I once ordered a mast from a well-known manufacturer and asked for cranes for the spinnaker halyard masthead blocks. I was told 'everyone' (i.e. the offshore fleet) now just had slots in the mast; that cranes just added weight and windage at the masthead. You only had to think about the halyard chafing the side of that slot if you kept the spinnaker up for a week to realise this was totally unsuited to ocean passage-making.

This focus on weight-saving is fine in theory. But if it means a fitting is only just strong enough for the task for which it is intended, it won't do for long-distance sailing. A few ounces saved can mean days lost on a long race if a spinnaker goes into the sea, which totally negates the benefit of the weight saved.

So, a final appeal to engineers and designers: please don't specify what is adequate, specify robust. It may cost a bit more money initially, but it is far better and far less expensive in the long term to have a higher initial cost for stronger equipment than a series of replacements.

THE RIG

Whether it's by tapping the wire to detect broken strands or tweaking backstays to tame weather helm, assessing the rig under sail need not be the black art feared by many.

Tuning a rig should be a science. Instead it remains largely a black art. When you have a long thin cantilever mast, you have to try to ensure that it is properly supported against the pressures exerted against it by the wind from the mainsail and the headsails, as well as pitching and rolling, and try to ensure it stays in column throughout. These stresses can be calculated, but those solutions are for a static situation, not the dynamic one when sailing.

The focus is on keeping the mast straight on either tack, but it is how you do it that matters. Start by getting even tension on opposing shrouds. Having the mast absolutely straight in the athwart line is one thing, but make sure the mast is upright otherwise the boat will have a different performance on each tack.

A simple method is to lock the main halyard and ensure that it touches each gunwale equally. Then set up the desired tensions. Remember that new wire rigging – and even rods – will stretch, so the initial settings will need subsequent adjustment and it may take some time to get it completely right. Like sails, they should be taken out in fair conditions to start with to allow them time to bed in properly.

But the initial set-up is only a small part of tuning a rig. When under sail, the windward rigging is working and holding the mast straight, the forestays are taking a lot of weight, but what is happening to the lazy rigging on the leeward side in the meantime?

If the leeward rigging becomes loose (and it usually will), it does not provide any initial support and that little bit of slack puts snatch loads on the rig as a boat bounces on waves. That in turn puts an extra strain on all the fastenings.

Think what you usually do when something is stuck fast – a good sharp pull will often free it. The same can apply with rigging. If the leeward rigging is left slack, the snatch loadings are a serious threat to the longevity of mast and rigging.

Just as threatening to the rig is work hardening the wire. Take a paper clip and work it back and forwards. It does not take many movements before it breaks. The same effect happens with wire rigging, although the speed with which the wires work-harden depends on their material.

Ordinary galvanised plough wire takes longer to be affected than stainless wires, but both are being weakened when they are allowed to move backwards and forwards, as happens when the leeward rigging is loose. An easy way to find out whether the wires have a broken strand, which is the first sign of a problem, is to tap the wire and listen to the sound it makes.

The strains on the mast change with the wind. Tuning the rig for a close-hauled condition is one thing, but the stresses change when the boat is off the wind. We are dealing with forces from a different direction and the straightness of the column, although desirable, is no longer so important. The mast now has to take forces from the beam or abaft, and we need to ensure it has sufficient support to deal with these tensions.

That is where our backstays and runners come into the equation, and the runners are the one thing we can adjust easily all the time. They are there to control panting in the mast and provide a brace against the inner forestay. The forestay is setting the mast bend.

But when you look at bracing a mast you quickly appreciate that if you apply tension in one place, it affects all the other segments of the rig. Try this by easing and tightening the weather runners while looking up the mast.

Checking the rake is also important. Always check the spreaders. If they are swept back, then, when you loosen the forestays or tighten the backstays, the shrouds will become loose.

If the mast is raked back, weather helm will be reduced, a useful point to remember if your boat has too much. Rake the mast too far and you can lose the feel from the helm; most sailors prefer to leave a little weather helm. Try it by letting go of the helm and the boat should come up into the wind. Then see the difference with different sail settings. Too much weather helm can mean the boat becomes unmanageable in a squall.

ATTACHMENT POINTS

How many modern yachts are really set up for anchoring or towing? All too often they are not provided with a good strong cleat or other reliable attachment point.

The prevalence of more frequent and stronger winds around our coastline means we should double check on how we secure our yachts. Most yachts spend most of their lives moored to a pontoon, pile or buoy and you would expect to see some fairly sensible and reliable equipment employed to ensure their safety – yet to look at them you would never believe it.

The smartest rope is used for sheets, the thought that goes into winch positions and sheet leads take precedence over the placing of the humble mooring cleats. It is illogical, can be dangerous and, if the weather continues to get worse, it will lead to an increase in damage and loss.

Take a look at the boats parked up in a marina; how many have a really strong cleat for the anchor chain or for a tow if necessary? Far too often the manufacturers or owners feel they can run a line round the mast when they are going to experience a heavy pull forward, but at best this will damage the mastcoat, at worst the mast itself.

Frequently, too, the cleats are placed where they cannot have the secure fixing that is so essential and are thus likely to be pulled out at some inconvenient moment.

The anchor is our last resort when things go wrong. A vessel that loses its mast can anchor, one that has an engine failure can anchor and be safe until the problem is resolved or help arrives. In bad weather we may have to seek shelter where there are no marinas or buoys in which case we shall need to use the anchor.

If we are cruising and have anchored close to a shipping channel, the anchor should take the forces exerted when a bow wave comes over. But will it? We have rules covering the weight of anchor a boat should carry, also the size and length of chain, but nowhere does a rule state a requirement for the strength of the attachment point on board.

This was all brought home recently when out sailing off Cuba. We received a message that one of our sister yachts had lost engine power as fuel was not getting through the injector pump. She was not in any danger, there was 25 knots of wind and the yacht was sailing comfortably, but getting back to the marina did present a problem.

The entrance through the beach is very narrow and only 3m deep. With a north-easterly wind, a large surf breaks across it and the swell reduces the depth in the troughs. Add to this a west-going current and the skipper was understandably unwilling to attempt passage by sail. We would have to tow them in.

We rigged a bridle over the stern, through the fairleads, back to the primary winches. Our kedge anchor warp was attached to this with a bowline and then flaked to avoid tangles. The heaving line was prepared and attached to the warp. We did not have a rubber tyre to take the snatches out of the tow, nor was there time to get out the anchor chain as dusk was falling – only one of the channel lights was working and we wanted to get through before it became dark.

The other boat headed out a mile offshore to give us sea room in case we needed a couple of attempts and then we closed in from windward under power. The heaving line landed across their deck first time and we motored slightly ahead.

They hauled in the warp, took it through the gammon plate and onto a very sturdy cleat. Gently we took their weight and turned through the wind so we could line up the channel half a mile out with time to make an allowance for leeway and drift. We both passed through unscathed.

A perfectly normal manoeuvre. The boats had the necessary equipment and there were no difficulties. In particular they had a large and well anchored cleat forward which could take the surges and snatching of the tow line that was inevitable in the lumpy seas.

THE ANCHOR & ITS CHAIN

On many boats these days the anchor is rarely
used, but that is no excuse not to check both it and
the cable thoroughly at the start of the season.

As we begin another season, one of the items that must not be left off
the checklist when commissioning is the anchor and its cable. The
anchor is such a fundamental part of the boat, used less these days as
most boats moor to berths, but nevertheless it is a vital piece of the boat's
safety equipment. When the engine breaks down, or the boat is drifting
onto a lee shore, the anchor is the first thing to deploy, and it is in those
circumstances that it needs to be dependable and quickly accessible.

The reason why an anchor tends to get less attention than it deserves
is because it is heavy and uncomplicated and rarely gives any trouble.
Nevertheless it should be given a good inspection before being stowed
for the season. There are few moving parts so it is easy to check for wear.
In practice, unless the anchor is used almost daily, most will last the life
of a boat.

The cable is a bit more vulnerable and the joining shackles are always
worth a check for tightness, rust or distortion, and the mousing on the
shackle pin should be renewed to prevent it coming loose, even if it looks
all right.

There should always be chain on the anchor, both the main anchor
and the kedge. Even if rope is being used as part of the cable, the first
10m should be chain. Weight is needed to ensure that the shank of the
anchor is pulled horizontally on the bottom and not lifted. If the shank

lifts, the anchor is more likely to lose its grip and drag. This is the part of the anchor cable that is pulled around on the bottom as the boat yaws or swings to a changing tide, and if the cable were rope it could get chafed by any obstructions such as rocks, stones or anything with a sharp edge that has been dumped.

The chain also provides a catenary through its weight, which acts as a spring to remove the jerking if the boat surges. It is those surges, when the anchor cable becomes taut, that frequently cause the stock to be lifted and can cause the anchor to break out.

Where rust is showing through the galvanised surface of the anchor or chain, take a wire brush to it and paint it quickly afterwards with something like red lead. Even if it doesn't preserve the cable it will keep rust out of the chain locker.

The weight of the anchor depends on its type and the weight of the boat, not the boat's length. For example, a boat weighing ten tons would require a 35lb CQR anchor, and seven-sixteenth inch diameter chain. On *Suhaili*, which weighs just under ten tons, I have a 35lb CQR as the main anchor attached to 10m of half-inch diameter chain and then 40m of seven-sixteenth chain for the remainder. The half-inch chain is slightly oversize, but it is weight where I want it for a peaceful night.

The generally accepted minimum amount of chain to lay out is three times the depth of water at high tide. This may be suitable in a nice safe anchorage, but if the boat is anchored in a place with strong tides, or where the winds are strong or gusting, it would be sensible to put out more chain. Being able to measure out the chain laid can be done by eye, but that is not recommended.

The chain should be marked at intervals in a way that can be easily seen and recognised. Choose a length that is practical, say 10m, and then decide on an obvious method of marking the chain at that point. The simplest system is to paint one link at 10m, two links with an unpainted link between at 20m and so on. But any system that works for you is all right; what matters is easy identification, by day or night.

Before stowing the cable, lash the bitter end to something firm and strong within the boat. There is nothing worse or more embarrassing than watching the bitter end of your anchor cable disappearing overside.

And make sure your anchor light is working and that you have an anchor ball aboard.

ANCHOR EQUIPMENT

In our enthusiasm for high-tech gizmos, we ignore the traditional techniques at our peril – as the old folklore over anchoring proves, there's method behind what seems madness in old seamanship.

Where do you put the hawse for the anchor? An obvious question, right? After all, on most yachts the gammon plate is at the bow and there's a roller for the anchor chain. Question answered.

But I was looking at some drawings for a new boat design and noticed that to avoid the bowsprit, the anchor hawse has been put on the starboard bow. Was the boat intended for the southern hemisphere? I asked.

It is not a seaman's folklore wrapped in misty tradition that states the first anchor you let go in the northern hemisphere is that on the port side of the bow. Like most boaty things that have been handed down over the centuries, there is a very practical reason why you would use your port side first.

We have known about weather fronts since the beginning of the last century. Before that seaman did not know this theory, but they did know that at some point in a south-westerly blow, a line of dark cloud with rain would appear and the wind would veer sharply to the north or north-west.

Nowadays, we know the passing of the cold front and we associate it with sharp increase in wind strength. If a boat has been lying to an anchor and it begins to drag and letting out more chain cable is not sufficient to stop the dragging, the next thing you do is to drop another anchor.

If you have started out by dropping your starboard anchor, when you subsequently let go of the port one, as the wind veers the boat will swing round the port anchor and chain. If you want to let go more chain on each anchor, the port chain can end up beneath the bow as well.

The objective of this preplanning is to avoid the anchors fouling each other, which can greatly reduce their grip and also make their recovery a much more complicated task.

In the southern hemisphere, however, the weather systems are reversed. So, if the boat is south of the Equator, you would let go the starboard anchor first, so that the port one would swing clear should it be necessary to deploy it too.

One of the initial reasons for having an anchor buoy was to allow crew to pinpoint exactly where the anchor was lying, something that could be especially useful when two hooks were down. A buoy has the added value that it allows other sailors to visualise where your chain is lying and avoid anchoring over it, with all the tangle that involves. It also means that if the cable parts or has to be let go for any reason, you know where to return to recover the anchor and cable.

Anchors and their cables remain as relatively expensive as they always have been; both are sufficiently pricey items that you only really want to pay for once, then replace them as wear (not incidents) dictates. So it seems strange that you seldom see anchor buoys these days – in fact I doubt that many boats carry them.

I suspect the reason for this is that buoys can be cumbersome. Yet they don't have to be large. They used to be made of wood that was painted red or green as appropriate, then secured to the anchor by a coir rope because it was light. Today we would probably use polypropylene because I have not seen coir ropes in ages, except Africa and India.

Today the buoy could be one of those mooring recovery buoys. I, for one, wish I had used one on a trip to Greenland. We were in a fjord just inside Cape Farewell, located to windward of the pack ice with the wind gusting around 55 knots plus.

Suddenly, our heavy anchor cable snapped. The only way to get out of this situation was to motor downwind until we had sufficient way on to get around. Then just before we ran into the ice, we headed back into the wind, with the speed reduced to less than a knot. Later we went back to try to retrieve the anchor. Except we could not find it – something an anchor buoy would have resolved easily and cheaply.

So here's a word of wisdom to all nautical gear manufacturers: before inventing a new method of doing anything on board, it's worth finding out why sailors had done it in a certain way for centuries. They did not have engines to get out of dangerous situations and were not just far more wary as a result, they were far more aware too.

LIFEJACKETS

It's a dangerous business going to sea and it makes sense to take precautions to minimise the risks. But there are always times when you should use your own judgement.

The sea is an efficient killer. We survive if we take sensible precautions and take time to practise and learn from our own and others' experience as a regular part of our sailing. If a situation gets out of hand at sea – and we have only to read reports of accidents to know that this happens more frequently than we would like – our survival depends on how we react. And that comes down to training and experience, not to mention keeping up with developments designed to improve our chances.

One of the most useful parts of the Sea Survival course, which everyone who takes a boat to sea should do, is the practical use of a liferaft. We all carry them, but how many have actually deployed one and know what equipment comes with it, or how to use it properly.

Boarding a liferaft is not always easy, but at least the course teaches you how to do it. That well-known axiom that you should step up into a liferaft still holds good, but if you do jump down onto one, you must make sure you don't damage it in the process.

Of course, you will be wearing a lifejacket at the time you abandon your boat. It might well be in a storm or maybe it's a flat calm and the abandonment is caused by a fire or some other event. The question of whether to wear a lifejacket when out sailing has become an issue recently. It is easy to take the minimum-risk option and decree that you should wear one all the time whenever out sailing, and it is hard to produce arguments against that, as it cannot be proved wrong.

A lifejacket cannot work unless it is worn, but its only value comes when a person falls overside. That risk comes without warning, a sudden lurch of the boat when you are standing and your centre of gravity is too high; the boom swinging across and taking you overside, as happened to Eric Tabarly; a spinnaker sheet suddenly tightening and catching you under the stomach and throwing you over, as happened to one of my crew in the 1977 Whitbread Race (we got him back); the falling overside of a crew member who has gone aft to attend to a call of nature – and how many bodies have been recovered with their flies undone? The risk is real and always there.

Wearing a lifejacket is like wearing a car safety belt. In most incidents it does its job, at least in enough of cases to make it a sensible thing to wear. But on some occasions wearing a lifejacket can be a risk to life.

I was collecting a recently acquired Open 60 and went for a gybe. I was wearing my lifejacket. The boat heeled over far further than I was anticipating and I was thrown down to the leeward guardrail. At that point, with water pouring over me, the lifejacket inflated automatically and jammed me, partially underwater, under the leeward guardwires.

The delivery crew were trying to get the sails under control and with no one to assist me it was with great difficulty that I managed to fight my way clear, still underwater, against gravity, with the pressure of the lifejacket holding me in place. I would have drowned if I had not got clear.

Are we focusing too much on the last resort that the casualty will float after they have gone overside and not on avoiding the actions that can lead to someone going overside in the first place? Falling overside is usually caused by people forgetting or being unaware of risks on deck. Most are avoidable if the crew are experienced and alert to what is going on around them. You should not just practise man overboard procedures to ensure everyone knows what to do in the emergency, but also to remind crew to be careful and avoid falling overside in the first place.

So should you wear a lifejacket? My answer is: if in doubt wear one. I would not dream of sending an inexperienced crew on deck without one, nor people whose expertise I was unsure about. I think it makes sense to wear them at night, or in rough and dangerous conditions. But there are times when I find one restricting and then, if none of the other conditions are relevant, I do not put one on. It's a question of using your own judgement, something the Health and Safety industry hates, but let's keep them out of this one.

SAFETY HARNESSES

A man overboard incident underlines the need to be prepared, but proves that even the best equipment can have its limitations.

When anyone falls overside from a boat their life is instantly threatened. Getting them back becomes the priority, the quicker the better, especially at night or when the water is cold. Last December one of the crew of *Glasgow Clipper* washed overside from the foredeck. Initially the safety harness and tether held, but slowly the harness slipped until the crewmember fell into the sea and disappeared astern.

Quick reactions, pressing the MOB button instantly and getting the engine started so the boat could manoeuvre back as speedily as possible, meant that the casualty was not far from the boat, but at night impossible to see. A powerful torch found the retro reflective patches on his jacket, the torch then failed, but the boat was close enough to be conned to weather so it drifted down on the casualty who was heaved aboard. The whole incident only took nine minutes, a remarkably short time and a credit to the crew's reactions. The speed of his recovery probably saved his life and shows the importance of training for incidents like this so the crew know what needs to be done and do it calmly and effectively.

Yet what concerned me was the fact that while hanging overside, with fellow crew members trying to get his tether onto the harness to provide another safety line and grab the harness, the whole lifejacket and harness had slipped off. The harness is a good make, made to the EN standard, but with an additional crutch strap and hood.

Back at Clipper Ventures we started a series of tests, hanging people in identical harnesses and seeing whether they could fall out. The answer is: they can in certain circumstances. Provided the crutch strap is secure, the harness will not ride up. It might become a bit painful, but the person stays in the harness. Without the crutch strap, if the wearer has their hands above their head, which is likely if they are stretching upwards to grab someone on the deck or even the gunwale, the harness holds up to a point, but if the chest/waist band is not sufficiently tight it will creep upwards. If the wearer is wriggling, this happens more quickly.

There appears to be another factor at work as well. Most safety harnesses are clipped together by pushing one metal buckle through another. When the strap is relatively tight, the pressure of the 'outer' buckle over the adjustable strap tends to keep the strap trapped, but if the strap is loose around the waist the buckle does not grip so effectively and the strap can slowly loosen. The more it is loosened the more easily it is going to loosen.

When we came to examine the actual harness that had been used, we discovered that the clip that holds the crutch strap to the harness had broken. It was a partial break. It would hold firmly if put in one way, but if reversed it pulled out easily. What was confusing was that both ways the clip connected with a firm click, which made one think it was safely locked. What matters here is that without the crutch strap the harness is less effective and could have proved fatal.

There are three fundamental lessons to be learned from this incident. The first is that the waist strap on a safety harness must not be left loose, it has to be tightened to the point where you can just get a closed fist between the strap and your chest. The second is that the plastic slips on crutch straps, which are tested to 200kg, need to be checked each time they are connected – and they must be connected. The third shows how important it is for a crew to know and practise the man overboard procedure so they all understand what is required to get a casualty back quickly.

This is not an occasion for specialisation, this is something every crew member must completely understand. Accidents will happen at sea and losing someone overside is one of the most frightening. It is never time wasted to go through the drill at the beginning of a voyage, if nothing else, to remind the crew not to fall overside!

THE LIFERAFT & SEA SURVIVAL COURSES

Your chances of survival will be slimmer if the first time you see a liferaft inflated is when you step into it in anger! Sea Survival courses are available, so why not take one?

The debrief of the three survivors of the recent incidents in the Southern Ocean by the Australian Maritime Safety Services makes sobering reading and highlights a number of shortcomings.

None had done a course on survival and only Tony Bullimore had launched a liferaft before, but he could not get at his on this occasion. Two liferafts were lost when they were torn away by the seas because the users attached the painter to the grablines and not to the strongest point. One overturned and the yachtsman had difficulty righting it, partly because he did not know how to do it properly.

They were unfamiliar with the rafts they had to use, and when you have reached the point of 'last resort' and are abandoning your yacht in bad weather, it's a bit late to regret that you don't know what you are abandoning into.

The possible solution recommended in the debrief report is that 'evidence of capability to survive in a distress situation should be included in any application to participate in these races'.

The report is not just talking about how to operate a liferaft; it is also about other survival skills. These boats are in the loneliest place on earth, thousands of miles from assistance and, as we have seen, rescue – if you are lucky – comes in days, not hours.

The report suggests that the sailors should have a knowledge of Search and Rescue capabilities and procedures for the sea areas through which they are passing. This makes sense, and the information should be made more readily available to the cruising yachtsman, too.

None of the survivors knew that the standard procedure by the RAAF in these circumstances is to drop two liferafts tethered together. Once into the raft, one of the sailors could not locate the additional supplies in a canister attached by line to the raft: he thought it was a buoyancy aid.

Liferafts are uncomfortable at the best of times, so how do you survive in one for days in a cold climate while being thrown around by huge waves? Thierry Dubois solved this by cat-napping for no longer than 30 minutes and keeping busy with tasks such as mopping out the raft.

There is no statutory requirement for yachtsmen to do a course in launching, boarding and surviving in a liferaft; there is not even a legal requirement to carry one or have it serviced annually. The only organisations to insist upon their presence on private yachts are race committees. (If a boat plies for hire it is a different matter and the Marine Safety Agency becomes involved.)

The RYA has a Code of Practice, but that is voluntary. Liferafts are routinely carried by most yachts because it makes sense to have one for emergencies, but there is something illogical about carrying highly expensive equipment and not knowing something as fundamental as its capabilities, limitations and what it really looks like.

We learn to operate a radio and take an examination so that we can use the equipment properly; we take Yachtmaster examinations; we look at flares and rockets; we practise man overboard procedures, all as a matter of course. It is time we added Sea Survival to the list.

How many yachtsmen round our coast have actually climbed into a liferaft from the water, or even seen one inflated? The RYA operates a very good one-day course, available all round the country, which covers all the items the Australians were suggesting should be known by crews.

If cruising yachtsmen are a bit remiss, perhaps with just short coastal voyages never far from land or assistance, they don't give it sufficient priority, but this excuse does not apply to the real ocean racers.

Perhaps responsible race committees could start the ball rolling by insisting that, say, each boat wishing to enter its race or races must have at least one person who has completed the Sea Survival course. With larger boats, where more than one raft is carried, there should be some proportion introduced so that each raft would have at least one crew member who knew what to expect and could guide the others.

It would also set a very good example for everyone else to follow.

TOOL KIT

A jammed and rusty spanner is an inconvenience on land – after all, you can always go and buy a new one – but out at sea poorly maintained tools could be a danger.

Helping someone prepare their boat for an ocean voyage recently, I needed a large adjustable spanner to tune the rigging. One was produced, but it was jammed and rusty and a new one was being purchased. With nothing else to do for a while, and not liking to be idle, I asked for a hammer and a screwdriver, and began the patient process of freeing up the mechanism. After ten minutes it was beginning to move and, as we all know, once you start obtaining movement on a rusty adjustable spanner, the job is more than half completed.

The new one arrived before I finished and there was a job to be done. But I was frustrated not to get the old one working properly. The attitude seemed to be that the spanner was jammed, it does not work, so get a new one, instead of seeing whether it could be made to work.

Maybe I am getting dated but, when I first started sailing more than 50 years ago, if something broke we fixed it if it was at all possible. Buying new was a last resort as money was always scarce, but in any case we had been taught to take care of our tools, and it stood us in good stead. When you get halfway across an ocean and need to do an urgent repair, it is not the time to discover that the tools are rusted up and probably some are missing because they have not been put away properly. Try finding a chandlery in mid-ocean!

Another threat to keeping a proper tool kit comes from the volunteers who come aboard to help. They mean well, but you can spend your whole time following them around and putting tools back in the box, because they probably won't. The time spent looking for tools left lying around is frustratingly time wasted.

You end up wondering whether it would not have been easier to have done all the jobs yourself, rather than acting as a tool gatherer, and at least at the end of the day you would know where all your tools were. Then there is the item loaned to someone else who then fails to return it.

The boat's toolkit is a fundamental part of its equipment. A screwdriver and pair of pliers might be suitable for a day sail in a dinghy, but is totally inadequate for a larger boat even on coastal hops. To start, a larger rig is likely to require spanners not screwdrivers, and the spanners will have to be the right size.

Whitworth is not so common these days since most manufactures have moved to metric, but will still be found on older boats. An engine requires its own kit, and if you look around your own you will quickly appreciate that an adjustable spanner will not answer all requirements. That means ring spanners and socket sets.

When you need to replace an oil or fuel filter you need a proper filter strap wrench to avoid struggling with oily hands on a slippery surface. And while on that subject, make sure there are always spare filters on board. A diesel fuel pump will not function once it has water through it, and they are expensive to replace. The last place you want to find this out is when making your way into a strange port in strong winds.

But all these tools are only useful if they are looked after and we know what a damp, salty environment can do to steel. It may be inconvenient to get grease on your hands every time you need to use a tool, but at least it should work immediately when wanted, and you can always carry an extra roll of kitchen towel to keep your hands clean.

What do you have on board to deal with a piece of broken standing rigging? Have you thought this through and made sure all the items you might need are there? I know it is very easy to overload a boat with spares and 'might needs', but there are some obvious items. It is worth going round the boat and looking at everything and thinking what you might need if it failed. That can make all the difference between being able to continue a voyage or having to abandon it.

So before the season starts, and before setting out in your boat, check the tool kit, make sure all the items that should be there are present and oiled where appropriate. Also, learning how to use them properly will save you a packet on repair and tool costs.

LEADLINE

You might suppose modern technology had made it redundant, but until an echo sounder can also gauge the holding on the seabed there's always room in the locker for a leadline.

An old skill you don't often see in these days of echo sounders and GPS is swinging the lead. I suspect most yachtsmen don't see the need to carry a leadline anymore because it will hardly ever be used. Probably its only use will be to check the calibration on the echo sounder, which can be done as easily with any weighty object and a line.

Before the advent of these modern aids, a leadline was an essential item of equipment. Its use was not limited to discovering the depth. It could also be dropped on the bottom when at anchor with a bit of slack as a way of finding out if the boat was dragging. The lead would weigh 5-7lb and the leadline is made up of stretched rope.

'Arming' it with tallow in the hole in the bottom of the lead would bring up a sample of the bottom which would indicate a rough position because the material of the seabed is indicated on charts. In an anchorage this information could be used to decide how much chain to put out. Soft mud, which is poor holding, equals more chain. Holding on rock will depend on the anchor in use, but it might have to catch on something. Clay is good once you get into it and sand can vary depending on its density. Hard gravel, which can be found in fast flowing rivers, may be the worst of all because anchors can have difficulty penetrating to get a hold, particularly if the boat is being dragged by the current.

In the days when the leadsman would be in the 'chains', a platform placed outside the gunwale to provide a clear swing, it was necessary for him to call out the depth he found in a loud voice, so it would carry back to the poop. I find hanging onto the main shrouds serves me pretty well because if the boat is going fast you need to cast the lead well ahead, so that it is vertically on the bottom as it passes beneath you to give an accurate reading.

The secret is to swing the lead fore and aft and let it go when it reaches its high point ahead of you and allow the line to run out. To provide added acceleration at speed, the lead could be swung around through 360° but in inexperienced hands this often leads to it landing on deck, which can alarm watching crew! The line must be neatly coiled, so it runs

Depth	Leadline marker	Leadman's call
1 fathom		"Deep one!"
2 fathoms	Leather cut with two tails	"Mark two!"
3 fathoms	Leather cut with three tails	"Mark three!"
4 fathoms		"Deep four!"
5 fathoms	White calico	"Mark five!"
6 fathoms		"Deep six!"
7 fathoms	Red bunting	"Mark seven!"
8 fathoms		"Deep eight!"
9 fathoms		"Deep nine!"
10 fathoms	Leather with a hole in it	"Mark ten!"
11 fathoms		"Deep 11!"
12 fathoms		"Deep 12!"
13 fathoms	Piece of blue serge	"Mark 13!"
14 fathoms		"Deep 14!"
15 fathoms	White calico	"Mark 15!"
16 fathoms		"Deep 16!"
17 fathoms	Red bunting	"Mark 17!"
18 fathoms		"Deep 18!"
19 fathoms		"Deep 19!"
20 fathoms	Cord with two knots	"Mark 20!"

out smoothly after the lead, then the leadsman gathers in the line as it comes vertical, when it should be on the bottom. With practice you can feel when this occurs, but try it at anchor.

The markings on the leadline were for easy identification and were called 'marks'. Between these marks the leadsman would estimate the depth and call it as a 'deep'. They are measured from the bottom of the line and when this is tied to the lead the additional small increase in length is known as the 'benefit of the lead'. It's a few centimetres of safety factor.

For small-boat use, the fathoms can be replaced by metres because it means less rope and ties in with the depths on modern charts. But I have found it helps to keep the same marks and materials for identification as their differences can be felt at night in the dark. On the Mississippi steamers in the United States, two was pronounced 'twain'. Now you know where Samuel Clements found his pseudonym!

SEXTANT

The sextant is not obsolete! It still has many uses – and not just as a back-up to GPS.

Longitude has become very popular lately. What with books and a TV dramatisation, just about everyone has heard of the Yorkshire cabinet maker John Harrison and his creation of the world's first accurate timepiece.

Accurate time was the missing part of the solution to calculating longitude. The other part, a means of taking the altitude of a heavenly body above the horizon, had been around for some time, the astrolabe, cross-staff, back-staff and finally the sextant; the latter two also developed by Englishmen, Davis and Hadley.

Although we now have the benefit of the electronic revolution in the form of GPS to provide us almost instantly with a position and not just a position line, a sextant still has its uses. It is not just the back-up to the GPS, it can provide distances off prominent headlands or lighthouses, angles between headlands and, for the racer, a method of checking on whether you are gaining or losing on a competitor by measuring the angle between the masthead and the sea's surface.

A sextant is easy to use but for it be used accurately, care and practice are necessary. The basic check is for the index error, the amount the sextant reads above or below zero on its scale when measuring a solid line such as the horizon.

Set the instrument at zero and look at the horizon. If it is one solid line there is no index error, but if one half is higher than the other, index error exists. Not a problem. Move the adjustment wheel until the horizon is straight and note the reading.

If it is below zero, or off the arc, note it and add it to your readings. If it is above zero, or on the arc, note it and subtract it from the readings. You can remove the index error quite simply by adjusting the index screw on the index mirror, but read this up before attempting it.

There are other adjustment screws on the sextant to deal with the horizon mirror being out of the vertical or slightly off-line, but these are best left to someone who knows what he's doing. Find a friendly Merchant or Royal Navy officer.

Taking a sight is easy in port when the boat is not moving and is a good place to start practising. The secret is to make sure you are holding the instrument absolutely vertical. The way to check this is to swing the sextant slightly from side to side. As you do so, the angle you are measuring will increase. Thus when you have the lowest reading the sextant is vertical.

Taking sights at sea is more difficult because the boats movement makes steadiness essential and this requires practise. In a rough sea it can take time, not just to make an accurate measurement, but because the horizon may be obscured by waves.

If your height of eye is only 8ft above the sea, your horizon is only 2.8 miles away. You have to wait for your moment and then take the time. Some adjustment may be necessary, however, because that moment may coincide with the boat being on top of a wave so the height of eye will be greater than your height above the wave top.

A quick estimate of the height of the waves solves this. Divide it by two and add the number to your height of eye. In rough seas obtaining a really accurate reading can be a prolonged business. I once waited 25 minutes in the Southern Ocean before I had a reading I felt I could live with.

There are two ways to find the body you wish to measure. Start at the horizon at zero and work up to it, but this is often difficult, particularly with stars. An easier method is to start at zero looking at the body and then bring it down to the horizon, but use a powerful filter if using the sun.

Since the calculation of longitude is dependent on accurate time, obtaining the exact second you took your sextant reading is vital. A second out can mean as much as a mile error in some circumstances.

If you are alone it is easiest to count from the moment you took the sight to the moment you read the chronometer and subtract the amount you counted. However, it is far better to have someone watching the chronometer to take the time when you yell 'stop'.

SUN COMPASS

What did ancient seafarers use before the magnetic compass was invented 1,000 years ago? A simple, but remarkably effective device called a sun compass.

The compass is fundamental to seagoing. Its steadiness is a by-word for reliability enshrined in our language. It is hard to imagine life without it but what did the seafarer use before the magnetic compass came on the scene about 1,000 years ago? Mariners did not suddenly start crossing oceans when the magnetic compass arrived. The Atlantic had already been crossed, voyages as far as Greenland were regular, so what was the secret of the ancient's ability to orienteer their way across the open ocean?

The answer is a wooden disc, which used the sun's movement to obtain a reliable datum.

It is simple to create. Make a disc about 10cm diameter and place a small pin in the middle about 1cm high. The pin is called a gnomon. Lay the disc absolutely horizontal then spend a day marking the limit of the shadow of the sun cast by this pin on the surface of the disc. If you cannot be certain that the disc is horizontal and live close to the sea, line the disc up with the horizon. After the sun has set, draw a line through the marks to create a curve. In practice, a perfectly satisfactory curve can be drawn from marks made at hourly intervals. You have now created a simple sun compass.

The first thing you will notice is that the curve slowly approaches the gnomon until the sun is at its zenith then it moves away to the edge of the disc as the day advances. Thus where the curve is shortest points towards the north. (The reverse is true in the Southern Hemisphere.) It can be made easier to use for steering if the points of the compass are marked on it once north is established.

The next day, at any time during the day, place the disc so it is horizontal and twist it until the shadow cast by the sun coincides with the gnomon curve. This done, the position where the curve is closest to the pin will be pointing north. The time does not matter, but you have to ensure that you are using the morning part of the curve in the morning and the afternoon part after noon.

Reading the sun compass accurately might be a two-man job: one to sight along the surface at the horizon to ensure the disc is level, the other to align the shadow with the curve. To understand the importance of having the disc level drop one side slightly: it is immediately obvious that the disc must be twisted to bring the shadow back to the curve, which creates an error.

Because the sun moves relative to the earth or, in navigational terms, its declination changes, the curve you have drawn will only be accurate for a short time. The curve will last longest at midsummer solstice and mid-winter when the sun's declination is changing slowly but will have only a short accurate life at the equinoxes. Therefore, a compass drawn in mid-June can be relied on for at least a fortnight either side but in March and September its accuracy will be limited to only a few days.

In practice, this does not matter as much as you might think because any error in bearing in the morning is automatically compensated by an equal and opposite error in the afternoon. The other reason why a new gnomon curve might have to be drawn is if the latitude is changing. Each curve is set for the latitude in which it is drawn. If the observer moves north or south, the shadow will lengthen or shorten respectively.

The first disc was discovered in Greenland in 1947 but last year another was found in a Viking site in Poland. Both date to about 1000AD.

The arrival of the magnetic compass made the sun compass redundant, and being made of wood few have survived. But the simple technology works just as well today and is easy to use and remarkably accurate.

LOGBOOK

A logbook should not be looked on merely as a means of recording your noon position and cataloguing sail changes; it is a record of your entire sailing history.

At the end of the season I go through my logbooks and make an analysis of the season's sailing. Then I add it to the long shelf at home full of logbooks. They date from 1965 when *Suhaili* sailed from Bombay, and extend right through to last weekend's cruise.

They cover boats as diverse as a 92ft catamaran (the Jules Verne circumnavigation in *ENZA New Zealand*) and the Sail Training Association's topsail schooner *Malcolm Miller*, and every one of the over half a million miles I have sailed – with the exception of one race from La Rochelle to Gulfport, Mississippi, when the French charterers walked off with the book, even though it was written in English.

In that row of books is encapsulated my sailing life. The logbook is an essential part of the navigation equipment of a boat. In it should go all fixes, bearings, position lines – and nowadays GPS fixes, of course – course, error of the compass, speed, wind, barometer and weather conditions, everything you might wish to refer to later.

A good log should allow anyone to be able to calculate where the vessel was every few hours, thus enabling the boat that loses all power from its navigation instruments to be able to work out an accurate dead reckoning and get safely to its destination.

The Merchant Navy trained me to keep a log properly. They had to be accurate and no errors were allowed. If a mistake was made, it had to be crossed out and initialled, so that it would be clear at any enquiry that a change had been made.

But just because the log might be produced as evidence in the event of an accident does not mean that it cannot be written for general interest as well. Sightings of anything of interest should go in, such as ships and marine life, sail changes, anything the crew are doing about the boat – it all helps to recapture the flavour of a particular voyage.

My entries showed a noticeable change when our daughter was about 12 years old and to encourage her interest we took to selecting postcards of ports and anchorages visited and pasting them into the logbook where gaps allowed. If we visited a port more than once, the card had to be different, and then a competition developed to find the oldest or most amusing ones.

There is another note from that era referring to a blue-hulled 'ferry' with three cream masts sighted at anchor off the island of Rhum!

Such entries bring back happy memories and at the back, on a spare page, I have kept a record of the crew who have sailed with me and their addresses, many out of date, some only dimly remembered.

Some years ago, when I was researching a rather interesting case of an East Indiaman abandoned in the 1730s, I went to the East India Library in London and asked to see the logbook. After ten minutes it was produced – a large, leather-bound book filled with copperplate writing, but the entries were as clear and understandable as a ship's log of today.

The incident I wanted – the abandonment of Captain and officers, but not some of the seamen – appeared in less than three lines, but there it was, documented.

When we were organising the first BOC Challenge, we decided to give a valuable prize of a sextant to the writer of the best log from among the competitors. This was not just altruism: we also hoped it would give us some valuable quotes.

The winner wrote a fascinating log, a very clear and interesting account of his circumnavigation which must be a treasure to him now. The runner-up was good, and then there was a gap. The bulk of them were so-so, and the poorest came from one of the most experienced sailors in the fleet who confined himself to entering the date and the noon position only.

This was doubly sad as he had picked up one of his fellow competitors who had had to abandon his boat, and has no record of the incident. We had more information on how the situation had developed at Race Headquarters, but we could never have the full picture.

The Indiaman's little known adventure can be read 260 years later; the BOC rescue will probably be forgotten – just because the log was not kept.

PART TWO

SEAFARING

BOATS

"Maybe we don't need to keep these boats for any pragmatic purpose and so that leaves just the reason of pride in our heritage."

Robin Knox-Johnston, August 2006

BATAVIA'S LONGBOAT

One interesting thing about sailing the replica of a long-lost vessel is to realise how badly they sail compared with modern craft.

In 1629, on her maiden voyage, the Dutch East Indiaman *Batavia* went aground on the Abrolhos islands some 45 miles west of the Geraldton in Western Australia. Of 322 souls onboard, 40 drowned, but the rest camped on the island. Two of the ship's boats survived the shipwreck and the captain took the 30ft longboat to the mainland in search of water. Finding none, he sailed the 1,800 miles to Batavia – modern Jakarta – in 33 days, an incredible voyage at the time, which ranks with Captain Bligh's voyage to the Dutch East Indes after the *Bounty* mutiny.

In 2003 a replica of *Batavia's* longboat was built by the Geraldton Regional Museum and is moored just outside the marina. The exact dimensions and rig are not known, but the original ship's boat was known to be clinker-built and flat bottomed and probably had a sprit rig with a single jib and leeboards, in typical Dutch style, so the replica was built along those lines. If you ever sailed the Thames Barge then the rig would be very familiar. Steering is by central rudder, not an oar, and the replica has a small keel along her bottom.

What is always shocking with these replicas is to find out how badly they sail compared with modern craft and thus appreciate the patience and seamanship of the men who sailed them. That was all they knew, of course, so by them their boat was probably considered a good sailer and they sailed within the restrictions it imposed because they were unaware of anything better.

On my day out with the replica longboat the closest we could sensibly sail to the wind was just short of six points or about 60°. Hauling in the vang on the sprit helped a little, but not much. Add to this 10-15° of leeway and you quickly learn that working to windward is a long business and anything given away below the course has to be patiently recovered.

The speed was not bad, but the performance was hampered by this leeway. The moment water passes across the hull rather along the fore and aft line it creates drag. Anyone who has sailed a boat with a short daggerboard knows that the performance can be greatly improved with longer boards simply because it reduces leeway.

When we came to go about it was an iffy affair; sometimes the boat would tack and other times she wouldn't and we were forced to wear round. That puts a premium on ensuring that sufficient sea room is always left to complete the manoeuvre just in case it becomes necessary.

In the choppy seas created by south-westerly off Geraldton we found the forward part quite wet when beating. A certain amount of water came in through the hull as well, which would have been accepted 400 years ago as nothing unusual, but of course this would not have been a problem with a large crew and it never became threatening to us.

The replica boat has been sailed out to the Abrolhos Islands and the regular crew felt very confident in taking her out to sea. In the fresh winds we experienced she gave no cause for concern and at some stage perhaps they will sail her to Jakarta. Then we shall learn a little more about the perils of long-distance voyages in boats our forefathers accepted as the norm.

Meanwhile, the fate of the *Batavia* crew left behind was tragic. A small group left in charge in the Abrolhos Islands began the systematic murder of other survivors to reduce their numbers, with the objective of capturing the vessel they knew would return to try to rescue them.

When the captain did return, some two months after his arrival in Batavia, he found that more than 100 of his men had died. The arrival of the rescue vessel led to a race between the leaders of the mutiny and some soldiers they had isolated on another island hoping they would die. But the soldiers had found water and fought off attempts to attack and kill them. The soldiers won the race and got their story in first, and the leaders of the mutiny were subsequently executed. Only 68 of the original complement of 341 eventually reached their destination.

Other Dutch East Indiamen were lost on the Australian coast before it was worked out how longitude could be reasonably calculated, and some of the wrecks, including that of the *Batavia*, have been discovered.

CUTTY SARK

Watching new rigging being made for the *Cutty Sark* offers a reminder that rig technology has been a driving force in the evolution of sailing.

For me one of the most interesting recent developments in yachting is that rigging has become the province of chemists. Man-made fibres are now as strong as steel, but much lighter and not as susceptible to the work-hardening that causes failure in wire rigs. Consequently, rigs are lighter and taller without losing stability. But it is still worth remembering where we started from.

The first masts were poles supported by wedges or thwarts. Fairly quickly ropes were added to help support the masts and, being practical people, seamen were soon putting up more and more ropes to provide support for sails flown at more angles. When wire became cheap enough, it rapidly replaced rope for stays and shrouds simply because it was stronger and less susceptible to chafe.

When standing rigging was made from rope or wire it could be made up by any able seaman. This is no longer the case – modern rigging is a highly specialist, scientific process.

As the traditional skills die, I find it a huge pleasure to visit TS Rigging in Maldon to watch the new rigging for the *Cutty Sark* being made. The wire splices were proper locking splices. The main shrouds were whipped together with heavy seizing wire and all the wires were wormed, parcelled and served where necessary over a sticky mixture of lanolin and Stockholm tar, applied as a preservative.

Though not so strong, plough wire is more flexible than stainless steel, but has to be protected to prevent rust; if properly treated it can last many years. Soaking new wires in melted tallow for an hour then wiping them over with white lead paste protected my rigging for more than 16 years. The paste could rub off on your hands or clothes, mind. The same applies to the new rigging on the *Cutty Sark*, except that Stockholm tar does not wash off easily.

The new standing rigging is authentic and, if the ship were able to float, it would be as effective as that used when the *Cutty Sark* was running her easting in the Southern Ocean. When you look aloft, you can only marvel at how cleverly the rig was thought through; despite the apparent complexity, there is a simplicity and symmetry of the sort that you would expect from practical men.

Built in 1869 at the height of the Clipper era, the *Cutty Sark* was created when speed was essential because the first cargoes home bagged the highest prices. British tea clippers were not as large as the American ships built for the New York to San Francisco run around Cape Horn. But they averaged similar speeds, mainly owing to their better light-weather performance. But in the year that *Cutty Sark* was launched the Suez Canal opened and steamers could ship tea much faster using this shorter route through the Red Sea. The *Cutty Sark* was soon transferred to the Australian wool trade.

The epitome of the square rig, she incorporated all the developments that had enabled sailing ships to compete against steamers. You have only to compare the rigs of the *Victory* and *Warrior* to appreciate that merchant ships were increasing the number of spars to reduce the size of their sails, so they could be handled by fewer men. This also gave captains more options about the sail-set.

The interest from a purely yachting perspective is the link in time. Our sport was just beginning to move away from being a rich man's pastime when *Cutty Sark* was launched. In 1867, John MacGregor published his book *The Voyage Alone in the Yawl Rob Roy* and R. T. McMullen's *Down Channel* came out as *Cutty Sark* made her first voyage. These two books did a lot to publicise yachting and make it more inclusive. These two authors would have taken a square-rigger as a normal sight when they made their voyages in yachts no bigger than a large ship's boat. But it was the beginning, of both small-boat leisure sailing and yachting literature.

KATE

A 19th century story of a cruise in a 25ft yawl called *Kate* paints a wonderful picture of the harbours round Britain and the people who made a livelihood from the sea.

In 1869 one Lieutenant Edward Middleton sailed alone around England in 25ft 6in yawl called *Kate*.

The voyage was remarkable at its time and Edward Middleton was an interesting man. At 15 he had been packed off to sea as a Merchant Navy cadet on a square rigged voyage to Australia but, deciding that was not the career for him, he joined the Army in India.

This lasted a few years before he decided the army wasn't for him either. On a subsequent visit to Southampton he bought a copy of John MacGregor's account *The Voyage Alone in the Yawl Rob Roy* and decided he would go one better.

Although he had not intended to write a book, his first edition *The Cruise of the Kate* was published in 1870. I found a copy in that wonderful reservoir of books on boating. The Cruising Association Library, but it has been published again recently.

Middleton ordered a similar boat to *Rob Roy*, from Messrs Forrest of Limehouse, who had built MacGregor's boat. She was delivered two months late (heard that before?) so it was not until June 1869 that he set out.

He went around clockwise. His route was up the Irish Sea and then through the Clyde and Forth Canal, before sailing back to London down the east coast. His book is full of eccentric comment.

During the course of his various careers he came to the conclusion that the world was flat and damned the Astronomer Royal for saying differently. He was not an experienced sailor when he set out, and his descriptions of learning to sail the boat are part of the charm of his story.

Middleton seldom sailed at night, preferring to go into port and find a hotel each evening if he could, and usually hiring a fisherman or pilot to help him into port and find a suitable berth. The pilot books of those days were written for coastal sailing craft, but did not cover the requirements for a small yacht dodging along close to the coast, and he kept land firmly in sight whenever possible.

What is fascinating is his description of the coast and ports 150 years ago. We have become used to marinas, but much of the time he was having to work his way into small fishing ports with few facilities except the willingness of the locals to assist him. Without an engine, he had to get the tides right or row.

Covering the distance between Bognor and Southampton took him more than two days, much of it spent rowing as the wind went light, and he refreshed himself with half a pint of sherry. He would have been safer out to sea, as McMullen would have told him, as McMullen felt that the closer to the shore the more dangerous the voyage was, which has my total support.

He had no antifouling; the bottom of the boat was varnished and needed to be scrubbed about every ten days. He appears not to have discovered any of the approved antifoulings of the time, such as varnish mixed with iron sulphide, zinc powder and arsenic, or copper sulphate.

Some strange mixtures were in use, for example white stuff, a mix of resin, train oil (oil from whale blubber particularly the Right Whale) and sulpher known as brimstone. There was also brown stuff: tar; pitch and brimstone to deal with the fouling problem that is recorded as far back as the 4th century BC and continues with us today.

The three pioneers of modern cruising, McMullen, MacGregor and Middleton all made single-handed voyages at this time, and all wrote of their experiences. Much has changed since then, but the sea is the same, the rocky coastline and its tidal streams that Middleton describes are all still there.

Their adventures are a snapshot into the world when poor roads meant that much trade went in small sailing coasters and before engines and GPS made our cruises a lot safer.

Perhaps it was the fact that their voyages were single handed, therefore encouraging others to feel safe, or maybe just the publicity their adventures caused, but they created an enthusiasm for cruising akin to the awakening of sailing in France provoked by Eric Tabarly's exploits nearly a century later.

WHALERS

It was great fun sailing a Montagu K Whaler, adapted from the open boats used two centuries ago to hunt whales, and which was often used as a sea boat by the Royal Navy.

Like many in my generation, I suspect, when there were some 300,000 men in the Merchant and Royal Navies, our first taste of sailing would have been in a Montagu Whaler.

This development of the open boats used two centuries ago to hunt whales had to be a good sea boat. It had to be strong enough to take the forces exerted (including, perhaps, a blow from a tail fin), light enough to be easily rowed or sailed and highly manoeuvrable. It needed to be brought quietly to within a throwing range, when a skilled man hurled a harpoon from the bow and then slowly belayed the harpoon line so the whale would feel the full weight of the boat, then sometimes tow it at high speeds until exhausted. This was known as the Nantucket Sleigh Ride.

The type developed all over the world – New England, the UK, the Azores and many others – because it was so ideally suited to its purpose. The Royal Navy adopted them and it had become a standard 25ft double-ended sea boat by the end of the 19th century. Early in the 20th century the length was extended to 27ft and it became known as the Montagu K Whaler – the only significance to the K, as far as I can elicit, is that this was the identification letter for a whaler on the mainsail. Who Montagu was no one seems to know unless he was associated with the Earls of Sandwich.

Clinker built – except those on the RMS *Discovery* which were carvel as the landings of the planks could have caught on ice – and double-ended, the whaler, when not being rowed, became a yawl which set a jib, a loose-footed standing lug mainsail and Bermudan mizzen. A storm sail could be used as a spinnaker but later small spinnakers were provided. The jib had one set of reefing points, the mainsail two.

The mainmast was keelson-stepped with a metal clamp on the second thwart. The mizzen had a small boom and this was triced up on a topping lift when not required. A steel drop keel provided some resistance to leeway. The normal crew was six – a coxswain and five – and there were five thwarts, as it was pulled single-banked.

Nearly every warship carried one but they were rare in the Merchant Navy where the motor lifeboat was usually the sea boat. However, we carried one on the cadetship in which I served the bulk of my apprenticeship, because it was ideal for training and leisure – we would never turn down a race if opportunity allowed.

On one occasion, in 1958, when eight warships suddenly arrived in Mombasa, a whaler regatta was held in Kilindini Harbour, including two entered by the Kenyan Navy. According to my logbook, HMS *Gambia* provided the winner and we were 2nd, but there were suggestions that our whaler did not conform. It was probably lighter than the standard Naval issue as the chief officer had decided to remove its white paint and varnish it instead. Sandpaper was in short supply so we used canvas hose and sand which probably reduced the plank thickness.

Weighing 27cwt, they could be raised by handpower, 50 sailors running down the decks with married falls brought the falls to two blocks very quickly, but in the Merchant Navy, where such manpower was unavailable, we led the falls to a cargo winch. They weren't light to row, but far easier than the standard lifeboat.

Sailing was a joy, though, because they had beautiful lines and in sheltered waters would sail with the gunwale about 5in below the surface without a drop coming inboard. This was where the coxswain and stroke played chicken with each other, the one refusing to luff up, the other not easing the sheet when a squall hit, until, inevitably, the gunwale went further than 5in and something had to give or serious baling became necessary.

Whalers were still being built in the 1950s but later the Navy adopted a motorised version and even these are hard to find these days. Many Montagu Whalers went to Sea Cadet units, but probably not many remain in service now. The lighter, lower-maintenance, glassfibre dinghy has replaced them as a teaching tool.

SQUARE RIGGERS

There is a beautiful logic to square riggers and, when running before a gale with the side decks awash, there is no more exhilarating experience.

Eric Newby's book *The Last Grain Race* is one of sailing's great classics. Square-riggers were a rarity just prior to World War II and this book provides one of the few modern glimpses of what life was like in the great days of sail.

The knowledge that this was the ultimate school of seamanship caused me to regret that square rig training was no longer available when I was a Merchant Navy apprentice. The German Merchant Navy still ran square rig cadet ships, but they lasted only a year into my apprenticeship, withdrawn after the loss of the *Pamir*. (The same storm caught us homeward bound in the Bay of Biscay, when, in a never-to-be-forgotten night, our 7,500-crew ship rolled and pitched so wildly the main deck had to be put out of bounds.)

I did manage a stolen week aboard the USCG barque *Eagle* but the weather was frustratingly calm and gave no opportunity to experience what has always seemed to me to be the ultimate square rig experience, running before a gale as they used to when 'running their easting down' in the Roaring Forties.

Last month I finally achieved my ambition. We had just collected the Sail Training Authority's new 195ft brig *Stavros S Niarchos* from her builders and were taking her from Avonmouth to Weymouth. The trip was a shakedown and an opportunity for the crew of volunteers to learn their way around the initially bewildering mass of cordage leading from masts to belaying pins.

In fact there is a beautiful logic about square rig. Years of development as a result of its being handled by small crew may have led to a vast array of ropes, but their purpose, once understood, becomes clear. Nearly half are buntlines, used to furl the sail by hauling it up to its yard so no crew are needed aloft if sail needs to be reduced in a hurry. There is an established order for these and the clewlines, leechlines, halyards and sheets and, once this is learnt, the use of each rope and its belayed position is obvious.

Each yard has its braces and only the lowest sail needs to have its sheets tended when altering course since sails from the lower topsail up are sheeted to the yard below. The modern equivalent would be bracing a spinnaker pole, although gybing a square sail is far easier.

Square rig is not, as many would have you believe, nuclear physics. It's not as efficient as fore and aft rig when going to windward and we have yet to get the brig trimmed to see how close she will go, but it is remarkably safe and easy to manage and once reaching or running, the speed is quietly impressive.

As we came down the Bristol Channel we soon learned that our brig tacked remarkably well and manoeuvred more easily than the schooners she will replace, so we felt confident as we sailed round Land's End and into the Channel with a rising westerly wind and Gale Force 8 forecast. Before long gusts of 44 knots made a reduction in sail advisable and the watch went forward to furl the fore course, the largest and lowest sail on the foremast.

This sail has eight buntlines, enough you'd think, to bag it up quite easily. Not a bit of it, and by the time we had eventually furled it, our arms were aching.

But now she was down to a comfortable rig, something recognisable from Newby or Seligman – staysail and inner jib, fore lower and upper topsails and main lower topsail. Black clouds scudded across the sky, through which an almost full moon illuminated the masts, sails and tangle of rigging.

Our rolling cycle was still the ten seconds that had been designed; slow enough to avoid jerking people off the yards but quick enough to indicate a good righting moment. Occasionally, when there was a particularly heavy roll, the side deck filled with water, like a scene from a Montague Dawson painting. The bow was pitching down as the waves overtook us, sending a bow wave roaring out 50 metres on each side. We were averaging an easy ten knots and the whole picture was pure magic.

METRE CLASSES

I love the style and beauty of the yachts of
yesteryear and the fact that many of these classics
are still around for sailors to enjoy today.

Yachts can be beautiful as well as functional. As a generalisation, I don't
think anyone would deny that the present generation of yachts with their
vertical bows and transom sterns are faster than those of 40 or more years
ago, but I don't find them as pretty.

The classic yachts so beloved of artists are those with the long,
overhanging bows and sterns. The International Rule, in use until the
1920s, produced some lovely-looking large yachts. Thereafter, until 1937,
we had the Universal Rule of the J Class, perhaps the most photographed
of any yacht class.

While some of the many classes spawned by these rules have declined,
others have survived and are prospering. The Sixes and Eights are healthy.
The 12-metres had a place as the America's Cup boats until 1987, but they
aren't expanding now they have been superseded in that role.

To avoid the age-old question as to why a metre boat is considerably
longer than its description, the designated class length roughly compares
with the waterline length, so a 12-metre could be 22m long overall. This
has been a metre class year for me. *Sceptre*, which I skippered in the
Round the Island Race, is that length and weighs 37 tons, something for
more modern boats to consider when they ask for a quick tack. (I found
that yelling that I wasn't the owner turned threatening boat owner's faces
white and they tacked quickly away!)

Not so the 8-metre class. Having just returned from the World Championship in Hanko, Norway, I can say, without hesitation, that here is a boat that could persuade me back into day racing.

The fleet is made up of three basic types. The Moderns, of which there are about 12 in the world, have all the things you would expect of a modern 12-metre, including winged keels and sophisticated electronics. Indeed, they look very similar, with the long, flush deck becoming a sloping transom.

The Classics are the older boats that have added aluminium masts and kickers, plus modern self-tailing winches. The Classic Classics still have their wooden masts, no kickers and old winches, so the sheets have to be tailed. There was one gaff-rigged yacht which, although lovely, wasn't competitive. All the classes raced together, with the Moderns tending to lead the fleet around the course and the two classic classes never far behind.

Our team had chartered a Classic Classic, but the mast had broken before we arrived so I went along the pontoon looking for a boat short of crew. I was lucky, as the Classic *If*, owned by Peter Wilson from Aldeburgh, was short of a hand. So I found myself ensconced in a small cockpit with two others, where flying elbows as we tacked were a greater danger than anything else. We had two for the foredeck and the skipper at the back. It was a very congenial crew, who knew their boat and, as in any series, now and again we did quite well!

The metre boats are long, narrow and deep. The 8-metres would probably sleep four or five people and a stove and heads are included. They are a more civilised form of the Dragon: big enough to live aboard and sail around the coast. Some have gone much further afield and even if it's not the height of comfort, it was more than bearable.

The crews are comparatively small. Compared with a modern yacht with similar-size sail plan, an 8-metre will have a smaller crew, with a maximum of seven and more probably six in total. The fleet amounted to about 20 yachts and we raced each day just out at the entrance to Oslo Fjord. There was entertainment every evening and we Brits appreciated the loss of *Britannia* all the more as King Harald had brought his Royal Yacht to the regatta and entertained all the crews aboard.

The atmosphere was friendly and rivalries were civilised. Perhaps one of the best memories was coming ashore after the last race and seeing the

King, having won his class, sitting on the club patio with his crew, beer can in hand. It was this sort of relaxed friendly occasion that makes you think this is what yacht racing should be about and that you'd like to do a bit more of it.

CLASSIC BOATS

With 60 immaculate craft from family pilot
cutters to Charles Nicholson's gaff cutter *Marigold*
and the 35m Fife *Cambria*, Monaco's Classic Boat
Week is the best sort of museum of sail.

If it is possible to bring together the yachting legacy of the past 120 years, the Classic Boat Week in Monaco is probably the nearest we can get. Organised by the Yacht Club de Monaco every two years, the event this year saw some 60 historical yachts, both power and sail, in the port.

But the real treat was to see them out racing each day. The sight of all these yachts, dating back as far as 1882, is one that would gladden the eye of any sailor. They may not have the speed of a modern yacht. They are a lot heavier for a start, and we have also learnt a lot about moving hulls through the water in the intervening years. But the gaff rig does provide a very large sail area.

In addition, this regatta is a history of yachting afloat because most of the yachts have been faithfully restored, so we are seeing them as they originally appeared. The rigging and systems for handling the sails are as they were when built. Such is the enthusiasm of the crews that they are sailed as they were too, and coming aboard is like stepping back in time. One has to wonder whether these boats were so lovingly maintained in their heyday because the enthusiasm of their crews and the attention to maintenance is phenomenal.

It makes such a welcome contrast with the rather sterile displays of boats in museums. These boats are living, used the way they were meant to be. Most importantly, they are showing us how they were meant to be sailed, so are preserving (or reviving) the skills of an earlier time.

Boats cannot be kept in their original condition if they are to be properly preserved. All need bits and pieces to be replaced during their lives, but they remain the boats they were meant to be if they are kept sailing and maintained.

Pride of place in the Monaco fleet had to go to the three-mastered schooner *Creole*. But *Marikita*, *Cambria* and *Moonbeam*, all restored, remind us of the glory of the great gaff-rigged yachts that only existed in sepia photographs 30 years ago. This year also brought together four Fife 15-metres for the first time in a century. *Mariska*, *Hispania*, *Tuiga* and *The Lady Anne* were all built to the International Rule of 1907 between 1908 and 1912.

The rule does not measure the length of the boat, although it approximates to its waterline length. As a rough rule, the length of the boats in the metre classes is twice their class length, so a 15-metre will be close to 30m (98ft) LOA. The result is a beautiful yacht with large overhangs fore and aft. But if you think that is large then Fife's *Cambria*, 115ft on deck, is even more impressive.

The big boats were usually daysailed 100 years ago, but elegant interiors were not uncommon. Crews were paid and large because there were no winches, only tackles to operate sheets and runners. Sometimes a tackle had to be attached to the hauling part of the mainsheet to create a sufficient mechanical advantage to trim the huge mainsails. The crew were housed in far less comfortable quarters forward. Core crews are still paid today, but their accommodation is often better than that on a family yacht.

While the large cutters and schooners drew most attention, the smaller yachts were well worth your time. Perhaps my favourite was *Marigold*, a gaff cutter, designed by Charles Nicholson and built in 1892, now lovingly restored. What I like about these old smaller yachts, which bear a strong resemblance to the sailing fishing boats and pilot cutters of their time, is that the whole deck can be used by the crew and its low bulwark makes it feel more enclosed and dry. On most modern yachts the only area that the crew can comfortably use is the cockpit and the rest of the deck is used only when handling sails.

DUNKIRK LITTLE SHIPS

It was a stirring experience to be part of a flotilla of 65 boats of all sizes commemorating the 65th year of the Dunkirk Little Ships.

Sixty-five years ago, about 800 yachts and small craft made their way 40 miles across the Channel to assist with the evacuation of most of the British army and some 80,000 French soldiers from Dunkirk. The evacuation has often been described as a miracle – Churchill envisaged a success if 40,000 troops could be pulled out, so returning over 335,000 men was a relief to a country girding for war and short of trained men.

The years have winnowed away at the small craft that helped create the miracle, but in May 64 evacuation veterans commemorated this part of yachting history by sailing to Dunkirk, led by the Admiral of the Association of Dunkirk Little Ships, Raymond Baxter OBE, in his small motor cruiser *L'Orage*, the only boat to have returned for every reunion.

The steam tug *Challenge* is not really a part of yachting history, but she is one of the few survivors, having made three trips during the evacuation, towing barges and small craft to lift men from the beaches once the moles had become too clogged with wrecks to allow further removal from the port. In recognition she is a full member of the Association of Dunkirk Little Ships and she was my steed, the largest vessel in the fleet with by far the noisiest steam whistle. She is now owned by Dunkirk Little Ships Restoration Trust.

Our fleet formed up off Ramsgate, in columns of four and, escorted by *HMS Severn*, set out across the traffic separation lanes. The wind rose to about Force 5. On a 230-ton tug this presented no problem, but some of the light Thames river launches looked far less happy once we cleared the lee of South Foreland.

What is staggering is just how unsuitable many of the craft looked for choppy Channel waters. It is easy to forget that many of the Little Ships were River Thames cruising yachts and launches designed for the river above Richmond lock, not to venture out into the unsheltered waters of the Channel. But those were desperate times and almost anything that could float was pressed into service. The Admiralty requisitioned many, using local boatyards to do the work for them.

The planning started before the evacuation and was intended to draw on all resources but in the end the boats were mainly drawn from Southampton to Lowestoft. No one knows the true number that sailed across. About 700 are known, but there were others who were not requisitioned or did not bother to check in. They just went over, did what they could and eventually came home – if they were lucky.

Many did not return, some 200 were lost in one way or another – just a small marina-full today, but a lot of boats then. If anything emphasised the depth of the maritime heritage of the British and the grim determination of an island nation to help out in an emergency, it was these yachtsmen.

Being a part of this fleet gave some indication of what the eastern Channel must have looked like at the end of May 1940. The busy naval activity was missing, no rushing destroyers and MTBs, although we did have a veteran MTB in the fleet. However, 60 yachts in close formation forms an impressive crowd. A couple of boats had engine problems, but the Ramsgate lifeboat was on hand to give assistance.

It was probably as well we had no examples of the small sailing dinghies that made their way across to help ferry soldiers out to the larger vessels hove to in the deeper water offshore.

Dunkirk was welcoming. We filed into the lock and then through the basins until we moored in the old port, bringing a touch of brightness with the flags as boats dressed overall. Walking along the quay, you could appreciate the efforts that had been made to spruce up for the occasion; varnish gleamed, brass shone, hulls had the shine of new paint. Some are no longer British-owned, the Dutch and Spanish flags flew from a couple, but they still made the effort to join. It would have been a toss up who won a Concours d'Elegance.

Some said that this would be the last time that the Dunkirk Little Ships would muster and return, but they said the same in 2000. I suspect these proud veterans will sail again in 2010 and it will be a sight worth seeing.

LADY DAPHNE

Derek Ling was no ocean pioneer – indeed, he grew nervous out of sight of land. But sailing was the poorer for the passing of a professional bargeman whose seamanship and quick humour were of a class apart.

Derek Ling has crossed the bar. He won't be known in most sailing circles, but among Thames barge sailors he was a legend. He went to sea as a 14-year-old deckboy during the war and worked until he became skipper of a barge, which he sailed commercially until Thames barges were no longer competitive. It is hard to believe, but in 1945 there were still 400 Thames barges in commercial use. By the 1970s there were only about 50 and none of these was operating as a cargo carrier.

I first met Derek at St Katharine Docks in the 1970s when his barge *Lady Daphne*, was operating on charter business. Like all the professional barge skippers at that time, he dressed as if for farm-working, except for a jaunty yachting cap. Short and wiry, with an infectious grin and a broad East Anglian accent, he was the sort of character you could not help but like. Yet after a couple of trips sailing as his mate I also developed a huge respect for his seamanship and ship-handling skills.

It was not just the way he could steer a 100ft barge into a narrow gap with a strong wind and tide adding confusion, it was his knowledge of the Thames and its estuary. The Thames has a gravelly bottom for much of its length, which does not always give a good hold to an anchor, but Derek knew where the best holding grounds were all along the river, where we could anchor and relax knowing that our hook would hold. He sniffed out where he was in fog anywhere between Kent and Essex or Suffolk, whereas I relied on dead reckoning and later GPS.

When we took the barge to the first Brest festival in 1992 Derek wanted to keep in sight of the coast to Dover and then slip across the Channel at its shortest point so he could hug the French coast down to Ushant. He reluctantly accepted my plan of sailing down to Weymouth, then heading over towards the Chenal Du Four because he liked to be able to see land. His brow creased in worry once we lost sight of Dorset and all the way over he kept coming to the chart and looking at my succession of plots, but he perked up when we sighted the French coast.

And he could be mischievous. When we entered the Brightlingsea barge match, we anticipated light weather. I, in my innocence of barge matches, suggested we use the spinnaker and smuggled aboard a huge kite the night before departure, so, as Derek put it, the others would not see our secret weapon.

On a very slow downwind leg we hoisted this at the top masthead. The topmast bent alarmingly, but our boat speed improved and we found ourselves the winners of the match. After some celebrations aboard we went ashore to be summoned to a smoke-filled room and be told we had been disqualified. We were told it was our spinnaker. We pointed out there was nothing in the rules against setting additional sails. "Well, there is now," was the response. We told them they could not apply a rule retrospectively and I am still not sure whether we were allowed to keep our win.

Derek would squint at the sky and pronounce there was a cartful of wind coming or look at the mud at low water and if it was shining tell us there was bad weather on the way. I never worked out whether this was true or just an old bargeman's excuse to stay in the pub.

Perhaps my favourite memory is at his retirement party. Derek had a couple of whiskies and was in expansive mood about his experience at sea, which from his version, meant he had spent little time ashore. I asked him how, he had managed to produce 10 daughters and a son.

He smiled and came straight back at me: "Well, Robin, I used to send my trousers home to be laundered from time to time."

TREKKA

That *Trekka* is used and loved in British Columbia, nearly 50 years after she achieved the first solo circumnavigation by a Briton, shames the UK's attitude to its sailing heritage.

Tucked away in a corner of the marina in Victoria, British Columbia, was a small eggshell blue ketch with *Trekka* painted on the stern. At just over 20ft in length, her 68ft ocean racing neighbours, the Clipper fleet, dwarfed her when they moored up as part of their circumnavigation. But *Trekka* had something in common with them and is something very special in sailing folklore because back in 1959 she became the first boat to be sailed alone round the world by a Briton.

John Guzzwell is a Jerseyman, but after being interned in Germany as a small boy during the war, he served an apprenticeship as a joiner and then emigrated to Canada. Within a couple of years, aged 23, he was feeling footloose and decided to build himself a small boat with which to go offshore cruising.

Laurent Giles produced the design for £50 and *Trekka* slowly took shape in the lee of a fish and chip shop in Victoria. Rigged as a yawl and beautifully built, she looks remarkably modern in many respects, but her accommodation is tiny, especially as John stands at over 6ft. Sitting in the cockpit you feel very close to the water, but it is only the growth in size of the average yacht since the Fifties that makes her seems so ridiculously small today. Humphrey Barton had only recently crossed the Atlantic in a Vertue, so a few feet shorter did not seem totally unrealistic for a yacht taking on ocean voyages in those days.

John set off for Hawaii, via San Francisco, where he met up with a couple sailing their yacht *Tzu Hang*. The rest of the story is enshrined as a part of sailing history. John joined Beryl and Miles Smeeton when the two boats reached Australia, was with them when they famously pitchpoled on their way to Cape Horn and were dismasted and subsequently collected *Trekka* and sailed her round the world.

I first met them in Seattle in 1976. Miles could not be with us, but Beryl Smeeton, John and I enjoyed a most pleasant dinner together. That was the last time we saw each other until this May, when, seeing the boat, I asked where John was. Well, he lived not far away and was coming up in a couple of days to give a talk at the Maritime Museum of British Columbia. I slipped in at the back to listen to a most amusing and fascinating account of his adventures but slipped away afterwards as John was surrounded by people.

We met later that day with his 'new' wife Dorothy – new as far as I was concerned, although they have been married for 25 years – and enjoyed an epic reunion.

Trekka is now owned by the museum which has just put her back into commission. She is sailed regularly in the local waters, an activity that keeps her in good condition and well maintained. Wooden boats, unlike wood furniture, do not keep well if stored ashore as I learnt when *Suhaili* spent a couple of years at the National Maritime Museum. They are used to being wet, or at least in a damp environment, and if put in a closed shed for too long their planking will start to shrink. If left too long the wood will dry right out and not recover, and that is the end of the boat as a boat, so it was good to see *Trekka* still being used and cared for. John's book *Trekka Round the World* is still in print and is a wonderful account of a circumnavigation before the big explosion in yachting, before radios were commonplace and the world was a less-developed place.

We have not been particularly careful of our yachting heritage in this country. *Gipsy Moth IV* looked neglected and forlorn when she was stuck in concrete at Greenwich. Thankfully, she has been recommissioned and although she is currently being repaired after grounding in the Pacific, she is back in her element. *Lively Lady* is still working usefully, giving young people a taste of life at sea and *Suhaili* will go back in the water when I get the time to finish renewing her fastenings.

But what of others? Maybe we don't need to keep these boats for any pragmatic purpose and so that leaves just the reason of pride in our heritage, something which appears to be politically incorrect at the moment. But that is just a phase in our cultural evolution and we don't want to find that future generations blame us for failing to preserve icons of a great age in sailing.

LOCH FOYLE PUNT

As tippy as it is slippery, the Loch Foyle punt
is Londonderry's answer to the Brixham Trawler
and a revived local class is reason enough to visit a
town that is rediscovering its sailing past.

Tucked away on the north coast of Ireland, about as far as it gets from the Solent, Loch Foyle is off the map for most people. But anyone who wants to venture further afield should put it high up their list of places to visit. I went for the first time in July and had my eyes opened as to the changes that have taken place in the area and its potential.

For a start, the loch is huge; nearly 180 square kilometres, much of which is protected for wildlife. Second, it has some very friendly places to visit, not least Londonderry. The city used to be a naval base. But first the Navy moved out, then the troubles distracted people from the River Foyle which runs through the city.

That situation is now changing rapidly. The waterfront has been tidied up, restaurants have opened and pontoons have been installed for visiting yachts. Previous no-go areas are now on the tourist route and the city has some of the only intact city walls in Europe. Just west is Donegal, a part of the Irish republic but an easy one to visit because there are no border posts.

I write all this not as a travelogue but as an introduction. Most of us know that yachts developed out of commercial craft, but it is still fun to discover working craft that are now being raced as yachts. One such class is the Loch Foyle punt, raced by the Foyle Yacht Club just outside

Londonderry.

The club claims to be the only fortified yacht club in Ireland because its main building is a small tower built in 1608 (although they would like to move to a larger site where they could improve facilities). The punts were originally developed from the Donegal punt, which in turn was a diminutive version of the Drontheim, a fishing boat imported from Trondheim in Norway.

Donegal punts were built by local farmers, so that they could fish for salmon or gather seaweed to spread across their fields as a fertiliser. The Foyle punt became the workhorse of the local fishing communities around Loch Foyle. And just as working crews of Falmouth Oyster smacks and Brixham Trawlers used to hold races in their heyday, so did those of punts, encouraging developments and, eventually, some standardisation.

Clinker-built, undecked, 16ft long, with fine lines and a tall rig, the punts look similar to many clinker open boats. But they lack a keel, which makes them interesting to sail – it is inadvisable to cleat the mainsheet as they react very quickly to even a slight increase in wind strength. The crew consists of the helmsman, the middleman and the jibman.

Their freeboard is low and stone ballast is shipped to help the leeward gunwale from going under. This is dumped on the middleman's stomach; presumably the idea is that if the boat does capsize the middleman will take the ballast with him and lighten the boat. Certainly, the punts accelerate with any puff of wind. But they also heel alarmingly and capsizes are common despite the ballast.

One advantage of an open boat is that the ballast will drop out if it capsizes and inverts, and without the weight of a metal keel the boat will still float. But the punts still need to be taken ashore to be righted properly. Jibs are backed to get through a tack and gybes are avoided wherever possible. Anyone who has capsized a Laser while gybing will understand the sense of this!

The class is very active and the Foyle Yacht Club has about 20 punts, from one built only a year ago to one that goes back 80 years at least. Regardless of age, wood formers not drawings are used to create the shape. The punt class also has its own rules. For example, a glass of whiskey has to be taken before a race. This may account for the occasional exchange of blows when the racing is close but an occasional punch seems a small price to pay for the conviviality that flows from this pleasant custom.

SUHAILI

Coca-Cola proved ineffective. Vinegar only cleaned the edges. *Suhaili*'s iron bolts are rusty and replacing them is proving tricky.

Some years ago, as rust began to show through the white hull of *Suhaili* owing to the dowels above the iron bolts that held her planking to her frames, I decided it would be a good idea to replace the bolts. After all, they have been there since 1964. The problem was that the ¼in bolts had rusted themselves in, and as the rust had expanded them, they had become very hard to remove.

Banging them directly with a hammer sometimes worked. But as often as not, especially where their diameter had been thinned by rust, the bolts bent over. If they began to look as if they were being pushed through, they were in fact doubling up on themselves within the frames and becoming impossible to remove unless they were drilled out. This involves using a machine to create a rather large hole, which then has to be plugged or fitted with a new bolt; it depended on how much of the original ¼in bolt remained. Some looked almost new and some, we discovered, had rusted away completely.

So, work progressed excruciatingly slowly. *Suhaili* has 24 frames and on average there are 60 bolts per frame, giving us a total of nearly 1,500 bolts that needed to be replaced with aluminium bronze. On a really good day I might be able to tease out around six to ten bolts, and for three years I averaged 100 bolts per annum.

At that rate, years of work stretched ahead; perhaps as many as 14 before we could go sailing again. Clearly, that was not acceptable.

I mentioned the situation in this column some time ago and received a number of interesting suggestions. One reader proposed vinegar as the solution – apparently, in days past boatyards had used it to free up bolts. So, we tried pouring some down a small hole drilled alongside the rusted bolts. While it didn't free the bolt it did remove some visible rust. Another suggestion, Coca-Cola, had no effect.

Lubricating oil or diesel oil did seem to help provided it was given time to work its way through, but it was not a guaranteed solution. We also tried heating the ends of the bolts using a welding machine. The end became red hot and even melted, but the heat did not transfer right through the bolts and shift the rust, so that was another option struck off the list.

I was becoming desperate when someone suggested that we use an air-powered chipping hammer with a pointed end. To make this work, we had to drill into the end of the bolts to provide something that prevented the point from sliding off the bolt and into the wood. The vibration made by these machines is tremendous and the noise can be heard from half a mile away.

The initial results were less impressive. Often nothing happened on the first attack. With trial and error we learnt that patience was required. On some occasions the bolt would not move an inch for around five attacks, then would slip through on the sixth or subsequent effort.

We also discovered that, after this initial shaking, two people, working from either end of a bolt and hammering in turn, could eventually initiate a small movement and once that got started, they could loosen the bolt with each thump until it eventually came out.

With this method work suddenly accelerated and we set a new record of 60 bolts removed in a day. Admittedly that was exceptional, but we have had two 30-bolt days and 20 a day is now common. Where we have found the system really effective is on the larger diameter bolts, such as those that hold the deck stringer to the hull and frames, and the chainplate retaining bolts. *Suhaili* was built to the old-fashioned formula that a boat should be able to be picked up by her chainplates – I have craned her using them in the past. But these bolts, though still strong, are rusting and that is affecting the chainplates themselves. So, they are being removed and regalvanised.

We have almost completely refastened the stern of the boat, having had to remove the engine, fuel tanks and cockpit to ensure that we could get at them all. One frame has had to be removed and will be replaced. Then we have to start putting everything back, knowing that whatever happens, the stern of the boat will hold together.

Our target of being able to sail up the Thames for the Royal Review in June suddenly looks possible and at least gives our small team something to aim for. Now there is only one thing we would be grateful for – a moderate spring.

MOD70

I anticipated a white-knuckle ride round the Island aboard MOD70 *Foncia* at Cowes Week. Surely, given the foul tide most of the way, Michel Desjoyeaux wasn't after a new record too?

The invitation took a second to accept. Michel Desjoyeaux was bringing his Multihull One Design 70 to Cowes for the Artemis Challenge. Would I like to join him for the Round the Island Race? Twice winner of the Vendée Globe and holder of the record for the fastest monohull circumnavigation, Desjoyeaux, aka the Professor, is a legend in solo sailing and the MOD70s tris provide fast and exciting competition. Only two of the seven boats would be at Cowes – Desjoyeaux's *Foncia* and Sidney Gavignet's *Musandam-Oman* – so it promised to be a fascinating match race.

An attempt on the record, a time of 2h 33m held by the late Steve Fossett's *PlayStation* since 2001 seemed improbable when the date was set and there was no chance of waiting for the ideal conditions – a strong northerly or southerly. Nevertheless, I looked forward to an exciting sail.

We started at 10.00 hrs, heading west towards the Needles into a strong south-westerly and against the tide; it would finally turn roughly around the time we reached the Needles, so we would have the tide against us for three-quarters of the race.

Having played around with a reef in the mainsail, Desjoyeaux decided we could take the full main and *trinquette*, a large staysail with ambitions to be a jib. *Oman* started to windward of us and kept the weather gauge

155

all the way to Hurst.

Daggerboards in the outer hulls of these boats cant inwards and can be adjusted to provide the hull with a simple hydrofoil which lifts the leeward hull or provides less lift and more resistance to leeway. *Oman* is the newest of the MOD fleet and her crew were still experimenting.

But their experiments were making them more efficient to windward and they were ahead of us at Hurst Point and kept their lead until the tack to clear the Needles. As any Solent sailor knows, the waves can heap up off the Shingles Bank in strong south-south-westerly winds. I was amazed at how speedily these tris tacked, having grown up in the early days of big multis like *British Oxygen, Sea Falcon, British Airways* and *ENZA New Zealand*. On those boats, backing the jib to get us through the wind was normal. But the MOD70s tacked like a dinghy – usually. *Oman* went too close to the Shingles, tacked, hit a wave and was thrown into irons. We tacked inside them and got ahead. It had taken an hour to beat to the Needles; too long, we felt, for a record attempt.

Once around the Needles we really took off, hitting 33 knots at one point. The wind backed a bit, so we were close-hauled all the way to St Catherine's. We opened up on *Oman*, but she was still there pressurising us. We set a larger headsail. *Oman* followed a few minutes later, but we could not reach off fully as the wind had backed.

Suddenly, the weather was playing ball with us. We rushed up to Bembridge Ledge, kept the tack until the forts were clear and went about. It took us just an hour from the Needles to the forts, a distance of 28.8 nautical miles against the tide. It did not seem difficult; the boat just slid up to the high speeds and held them, though the occasional glimpse of propeller beneath the centre hull indicated we were pushing hard.

It was when I saw half a metre of air below the prop that I gulped slightly, but the crew seemed totally unconcerned. This had more than made up for our slow run to the Needles and now we only had eight miles to sail and 33 minutes to sail it. Perhaps we could break the record.

Being Cowes Week, the Solent was full of racing boats. The last thing we wanted to do was ruin their crew's races, but we were also racing. Desjoyeaux expertly manoeuvred us through various fleets to flash across the finish line at 12.21 hrs and 25 seconds, a total race time of 2h 21m 25s. Not to be outdone *Oman* screamed in only one minute, 28 seconds later. Both boats had smashed the record – not a bad little race!

RACES

"If something is easy it has no attraction and no satisfaction."

Robin Knox-Johnston, December 2010

CHANGES IN SINGLE-HANDED RACING

So quickly has technology advanced that sailing records are now shattered in the sort of oversized dinghies which would have made the doubting sages of the early Sixties splutter into their beards.

Single-handed round-the-world sailing has developed so much in 40 years that you could draw parallels with the difference between the Wright Brothers' pioneering aircraft and Concorde. The boats are vitally different and equipment, including electronics, has advanced in a way that could never have been imagined in those days.

The 1960s were the original golden age of solo sailing, when the foundations were laid for the modern sport. It was the decade of the new OSTAR, the single-handed transatlantic race, and two repeats, the event of 1964 introducing a French phenomenon called Eric Tabarly. With remarkable rapidity, these Atlantic races led to Francis Chichester and Alex Rose's circumnavigations, followed by the Sunday Times Golden Globe in 1968.

The early voyages round the world were pathfinding and proved that boat and man could survive a savage test for ten months. Yes, the Golden Globe was a race, but survival was considered paramount. Getting round non-stop was going to be the record and I was lucky enough to be the one to do it.

By the end of the decade, solo sailing was on the charts and in the 37 years since it has developed in a manner that could not have been conceived then. In part, this is due to the greater interest, with more people and more brain-power applied to make it both safer and easier. But it is also down to new materials, developments and inventions that have been applied to the design and build of boats.

There was no ideal of a boat for long ocean voyaging in the 1960s. You only have to look at race entries to appreciate that. Experiments were made with monohulls and multihulls, lightweight and heavy boats, long keels and fin and skeg, GRP, wood, steel and aluminium. *Suhaili* was considered unsuitable by most pundits for a non-stop circumnavigation and the general view was that multihulls were unsuited to ocean sailing and thoroughly dangerous for circumnavigation, but Nigel Tetley dispelled that myth in the Golden Globe.

This changed in 1982 with Phillipe Jeantot's *Credit Agricole* for the first BOC Challenge (now the VELUX 5-Oceans), which resembled a dinghy more than the accepted heavy ocean-going yacht, and this trend has continued. Wide, shallow, plumb-bowed, transom-sterned and, above all, light, the modern Open class boat is closer to a large Laser dinghy than the ocean racer of 40 years ago.

As for rigs, there was a general idea that a ketch was about right as it divided the sails into more manageable and convenient sizes and made the boat easier to handle and balance if the self-steering packed up. The sloop rig is now the norm, with enormous fully battened mainsails.

Sponsorship was not exactly welcomed in sailing circles. Chichester was criticised for having the woolmark on the bow of his boat, so the sport was out of reach for all but the wealthy. Although the first OSTAR comprised people who could afford their yachts, by the end of the decade new and younger sailors appeared who could never have participated without sponsorship. Sponsorship was not easy to find, though. All my savings – and a bit more – went into *Suhaili* and my efforts to find sponsorship produced only a £5 voucher and 120 cans of beer!

Windvanes were commonplace but the autopilot was not. It would not have been trusted even if it were because of its reliance on electrical power. Solar panels were not available, wind generators had not arrived and batteries were nothing like so light and powerful, nor could they be inverted without acid flying everywhere.

Masts were wood or aluminium, rigging was steel, stainless or galvanized. Sails were Dacron (or terylene as it was called) and stretched with use. They were tough and could be repaired with palm and needle, but at the end of a voyage they bore little resemblance to the pristine sails of the start.

Nor have the changes been all about the boats. Food came in tins before freeze-drying and water had to be carried or collected from the sails.

GPS has been a boon for yachtsmen, providing a fix every few seconds day or night, fog or clear, whereas navigation for the 1960s yachtsman had barely progressed beyond the methods known to Captain Cook. In practical terms you only really got the chance of three position fixes a day, which would take an hour or so to work out. If the sky was covered by cloud you could go for days without a fix, relying on dead reckoning.

Communications were haphazard at best. Flags and the Aldis lamp were still in common use, but obviously limited to line of sight. Beyond the horizon there was only single sideband (SSB) radio. Yacht sets were low-powered, their weak signals easily drowned out by those of larger ships. There were also heavy, used thermionic valves instead of silicon chips and were susceptible to all sorts of problems. Mine packed up after two-and-a-half months and thereafter I used an Aldis light when I met the occasional merchant ship.

Sometimes five hours of calling a shore station led to nothing except flat batteries. Faced with so much effort, often wasted, little wonder that most of us only bothered once a week. Nowadays you can communicate from anywhere in the world at any time using satellite and mobile Iridium phones. Personally, the thought of being at the beck and call of any phone caller when at sea contradicts the reason for going solo and removes the need to be totally self-reliant, but I concede it has its advantages.

Satellite communications also mean information can be easily passed back to the yachts, in particular meteorological updates. Unless you were a professional radio operator, no weather information was available in the 1960s because shipping forecasts for the high seas came out in high-speed Morse and had to be decoded as well. Fax had not been invented and access to satellite pictures was still a dream.

The advent of weather information and the improvement in the prognoses has brought enormous advantages. It is now possible to plan ahead and decide where to steer the boat to obtain the best weather for the next few days, which has made for much faster and safer passages. Previously, although the barometer's fall would warn of bad weather approaching, you never knew how much the pressure would drop, so what strength of wind might be on its way – and in the Southern Ocean that could be more than Force 10.

Communications also mean back-up. The modern solo sailor can get more rest and concentrate on sailing the boat faster if someone fresh and specialised is looking after the weather; the router has only appeared in the last 25 years, for example. Problems with equipment can also be left to the experts. It took me eight months to find the problem with my radio, during which time I had no contact except with some fishermen off New Zealand, and when I finally repaired it, I was not sure I had succeeded until close to home because, despite trying on the various frequencies in use, no one answered.

Circumnavigation times have come crashing down. A lighter boat with a larger sail area will go faster. And because it is lighter the strains are reduced, so lighter spars and rigging can be used. Faster passages mean less wear and tear, so there's no need to carry a lot of spares – yet another weight saving. *Suhaili* weighs just short of ten tons and has a waterline of 26ft. The modern Open 60 monohull has more than twice the waterline, weighs a ton or so less and carries four times the sail area,

Add the confidence factor – that the modern sailor knows the voyage is possible and is less hesitant – and solo circumnavigations now take a third of the time they did in 1969 for monohulls, a quarter for multis.

They are also safer. When you sailed in the Sixties you set out and nothing might be heard from you until you reached your destination. If you got into trouble, you sorted it out yourself or disappeared. This was not trying to conform to some Corinthian ideal. Barring the radio or a lucky sighting by a ship, there was no system available to alert anyone if you were in trouble – no EPIRBs or polling via systems like Satcom C or Argos. As a result of those developments, a number of people are alive now who would not have survived had they had the same accident four decades ago.

However, even if being able to tell the world you are in difficulties reduces some of the risks, the world still has to get to you. And whatever man may invent to make life simpler and safer, we can never control the sea. It is still its same dangerous self and it does not matter how sophisticated our equipment, how fast or tough our boats, how good the information we receive, the winds are still as strong and the waves as high, and meteorological forecasts are still a notoriously perishable commodity. We may have invented our way around some of the chores, made systems more effective and safer, but we have yet to create the boat that is absolutely unsinkable.

ROUND THE WORLD: SOLO OR TWO-UP

Two races set off round the world this autumn, both in Open 60s. But only one, the long-standing Velux 5 Oceans race, channels the Corinthian can-do spirit of solo sailing.

There are two round the world yacht races over the northern winter season. The first is the long-established Velux 5 Oceans race, which started life as the BOC Challenge in 1982 and has run every four years since.

Now in its eighth edition, this is a single-handed race and for this coming event it starts and finishes in La Rochelle, and stops in Cape Town, Wellington (New Zealand), Salvador (Brazil) and Charleston (USA). In the past it has started from Newport, USA, Charleston and Bilbao.

The other round the world event is a two-handed race first run in 2007, which starts and finishes in Barcelona. The Barcelona World Race has no stops, but boats can pull in for repairs.

Both events use the Open 60 class that was originally developed by the ten finishers from the first BOC Challenge in 1983. But there the similarities stop. The Barcelona race is for the latest IMOCA boats, manned by two professionals with sponsor budgets. The budgets need to be large – new boats cost more than £3.5 million each, plus there is the cost of a large support crew.

The Velux 5 Oceans could not be more different. It attracts largely Corinthian adventurers who want to step outside the box of their normal lives and take on something special. And a solo circumnavigation is very special; just 176 people have completed a proper one that goes south of the three great capes of Good Hope, Leeuwin (in Australia) and Cape Horn.

This is fewer than the number of humans who have been rocketed into space. Of these, 19 have been British Islanders, 17 of whom are alive – accepting Irish and domiciled New Zealanders as being in the geographical British Isles.

To keep the cost of achieving a solo circumnavigation to sensible levels, the Velux 5 Oceans has created the Eco 60 Class, which puts a limit on the age of yachts. There are also limits on the number of people allowed in a support team and restrictions on the size of the sail wardrobe.

There is a performance divide in the Open 60 fleet at 2003. Boats built since that date are more powerful and up to 25 per cent lighter, so faster.

In the Artemis race in 2008, for instance, newer boats were well on their way to the Nab Tower when the older boats were just coming up to the forts. Yet a close pack among the trailing boats made for exciting sailing. The boats built before 2003 also tend to be stronger – and well-tried.

Most important of all, older Open 60s can be picked up for less than 10 per cent of the cost of a new boat, making this pure form of sailing much more accessible to those without big sponsors or deep pockets. This provides an opportunity for adventurers and aspiring racers to access the realms of the professionals.

Two-handed racing is far more than twice as easy as sailing solo. Sailing in a duo is not just an extra pair of hands to help with the work and keep up the pressure when the other is asleep. It is about sharing skills and getting some decent rest when you can share watch keeping.

Tasks such as manoeuvring or changing sails are a lot of work when you are single-handed. Everything has to be pre-planned to avoid rushing backwards and forwards between each activity. For example, setting a $350m^2$ spinnaker without someone to help keep it clear while it is hoisted can be time-consuming and frustrating. And if that is tough, then getting the sail back down again can be totally exhausting – imagine trying to pull the sail inboard while also controlling the halyard on a winch 5m away.

For the true single-hander the lack of a companion does not matter. One of the reasons for sailing solo, notwithstanding the challenge of carrying out alone all of the tasks that are normally assumed by a crew, is the freedom of being alone on the oceans far from land. Storms can be planned for, but approaching a shipping lane or land is when being on your own really takes its toll – it is at this moment that falling asleep can pose a real risk to your own life.

So why do it? Well, if something is easy it has no attraction and no satisfaction. It is those days alone at sea traversing oceans that makes the solo circumnavigation the ultimate challenge.

VELUX 5 OCEANS RACE

I get a battering in the first few days of the Velux 5 Oceans single-handed race as storm force winds sweep the Bay of Biscay just after the start.

If a gale is forecast any sensible person doubles their mooring lines, or puts out more anchor cable and stays safely in shelter. When the Velux 5 Oceans race started we knew we were in for a gale but not a storm and certainly not one to bring winds in gusts of hurricane strength. It is worth remembering that the winds can exceed the average force by up to 40 per cent in gusts, so in 40 knots of wind expect gusts up to 56 knots.

We left Bilbao on 22 October and set off along the north Spain coast, a nice fine reach to start with. The gale was due the next day. The Open 60s are designed to be tough enough for the Southern Ocean, so a gale is manageable, if uncomfortable. The light ESE wind died about mid-morning but soon the wind rose from the south-west. Within three hours of the change the wind was gusting 42 knots.

I reduced sail rapidly in those three hours to just the storm jib. In retrospect, I wonder whether I should not have tacked, or worn round and headed back in towards the coast to reduce the fetch on the waves. The Bay of Biscay has a nasty reputation. It is wide open to the Atlantic and, when the winter storms start to roll in, it can be a very dangerous place. I was the most seaward of the boats and so the most exposed to the south-west and therefore receiving the largest waves.

As darkness fell on the second day the wind was a steady 45 knots but gusting much higher – the highest I saw was 72 knots. My main concern at the time was to keep the boat from becoming overpressed as you can never tell what damage you might be doing when she shudders from the impact of a large wave.

With the tiller lashed to leeward she crept forward, sometimes up to eight knots, which meant that, close-hauled as we were, when we ran into a wave she could take a considerable pounding. There was not much more I could do now except take down the storm jib, not a difficult job, but I left it set as, at that stage at least, I felt some momentum was helping. I stood in the cockpit for an hour or more just watching the boat's performance.

The rain squalls, which came every half an hour or so and completely wiped out visibility, seemed to be flattening the tops of the waves. She was comfortable most of the time, feeling underpowered and rolling easily with the increasing waves and this seemed safe enough. Also I had searoom, no land to leeward for 250 miles.

I went below for a rest, lying across the navigator's bench. The next thing I was aware of was a huge push, not a blow, and the boat rolling over to starboard. For a moment, I was vertical and worried about falling backwards as I had fractured my coccyx three weeks before and did not want to hit it again.

In what seemed a second the boat swung upright and I scrambled out on deck to check for damage. The windex had disappeared from the masthead and the other instruments were showing crazy wind angles.

Shortly after the roll the wind began to ease. By daybreak it was down to Force 4 and the time had come to get moving. I went to hoist the mainsail and discovered this was not going to be an option as a small section of track had torn away. I persuaded the sliders as far as the first reef to rejoin above the break, but it was clear I could not risk going into the Southern Ocean with a section of main track missing, so I reluctantly headed for La Coruña.

Alex Thomson in Hugo Boss and Mike Golding in *Ecover* had also pulled in for repairs. To what extent their subsequent problems were brought about by that storm we may never know – perhaps not at all. But Hugo Boss's keel failed four weeks later and the *Ecover* broke her mast shortly afterwards.

The boats are tough but either we are sailing them harder than we should or there are some questions to be raised about their engineering. The good news: no one was hurt and no outside assistance called for.

VENDÉE GLOBE

With the Vendée Globe drawing to a close,
Robin looks at the perils of the treacherous
Southern Ocean and the challenges facing the solo
gladiators in their 60ft chariots.

Northern Hemisphere winter is the season for round-the-world racing.
The reason is simple – it is summer in the Southern Hemisphere. No one
in his or her right mind would go willingly into the Southern Ocean in
the southern winter. It is a cold, miserable stormy place at times in the
summer and much colder, more miserable and stormier in the winter.
You only have to read accounts of sailors climbing icy rigging to furl
frozen canvas sails to appreciate how tough life was for the crew of a
square-rigger in winter rounding the Horn.

Nowadays we have far better clothing; sailors no longer work up
the mast and trips aloft are unusual; we have far better food to provide
energy; and it's possible to have instant communication with people on
land and at sea (something not possible even 30 years ago). But at times
when a square-rigger would have her decks swept by a Southern Ocean
greybeard, the modern yacht is so light it would be picked up by these
giant waves and tossed headlong into the sea.

Twenty yachts, a record fleet, set out from Les Sables-d'Olonne in
November last year for the Vendée Globe. This is a non-stop single-
handed race around the world and the start was visited by more than a
quarter of a million people. On past experience about half will finish. It is
justifiable to ask why the high casualty rate. Well, the main reason is that

these yachts are taking on the Southern Ocean and for many of the sailors in the race this will be their first experience of the gigantic waves that can be generated there.

Even for experienced sailors, the Southern Ocean is the ultimate challenge. The reason for those large waves is simple: the Southern Ocean is the only ocean that goes all the way around the world without interruption by land. The waves can roll ever onwards, but the good news is that the maximum size they can reach, theoretically, is 36.5m (120ft) high, so we're told!

The reason for these gigantic waves is due to the meteorological conditions. To the north of the Southern Ocean are high-pressure systems in the Atlantic, Indian and Pacific Oceans. Between these systems and Antarctica lies an area of eastward-moving depressions. North of these depressions the wind is westerly, south of them, to about 50° south, the winds are easterly. The secret, if you want to go east, is to keep between the oceanic high-pressure systems and the depressions. Too close to the depressions and the winds – and waves – will be too great and force you to go into survival mode and you won't make the speed you want. Too close to the highs the waves are smaller, but the wind will be lighter.

The Open 60 yachts being used by the Vendée sailors are among the safest yachts afloat and also the fastest monohulls for their length. The rules governing the class include watertight subdivision, and controls on stability, which include limits on ballast tanks. These rules, originally created by the BOC Challenge and now adopted and developed by IMOCA, have always been created by the people who take the boats to sea – the sailors. They have been upgraded since we saw Tony Bullimore's boat upended a few years ago.

No other class has so much input from the people who actually take the boats into the worst sea conditions in the world. It is no wonder that it insists on a test of the yacht's ability to right herself from the totally inverted position, with the sailor inside. The rules are simple, a few sensible clauses allow free rein within a length of 60ft. It is a growing class. There are more than 30 IMOCA-certified 60ft class boats in existence and at least five being built. There are some 12, with four being built, of the Open 50 Class. They have a clearly set out calendar: the Vendée Globe, 5-Oceans, the Transat, the Jacques Vabre, the Route du Rhum. The solo sailor against the raw power of Nature has always been attractive because, perhaps, like the games in Rome, there is a risk to the gladiator.

These yachts set out on one of the ultimate challenges open to sportsmen in any sport. There will be casualties, but that is because the course is far more challenging and has hazards that do not exist in the normal calendar of yacht racing.

200TH SOLO CIRCUMNAVIGATION

LT Cdr Abhilash Tomy benefited from better technology when he became the 200th solo sailor to circumnavigate via the three great capes, but the challenge is as tough as ever.

When LT Cdr Abhilash Tomy of the Indian Navy returned to Mumbai on 31 March, he became the 200th person to sail solo around the world on the proper route, according to my list. The accepted route is south of the three great capes: Good Hope, Leeuwin in Western Australia and, of course, Cape Horn. Only if a boat has sailed south of these has she faced the full Southern Ocean, which is the real test. A voyage that takes the sailor through the Suez or Panama Canal does not count.

My 200 total is for all sailors who have made the voyage whether they did it non-stop or with pauses; regardless of whether they were in a race and the time it took them. LT Cdr Tomy made his voyage non-stop and three years ago the same boat, *Mhadie*, was sailed the same route but with stops, by Commander Dilip Donde, also of India. This is India's first foray into solo sailing, adding to a very international list of sailors who have completed the voyage. The largest single nationality on the list is France, with 50 sailors. The British come second with 28.

I do not claim that my list, which starts with Joshua Slocum in 1896 and is published on my website (www.robin-knox-johnston.co.uk - use the site map) is 100 per cent accurate, but it is probably as close as there is. It counts each sailor once. If someone has made several solo circumnavigations they are ranked for their first one – others are recorded below. Notwithstanding round the world races, which are well publicised, the list's accuracy depends on the people letting me know of voyages that can be verified.

Having rounded in 1969, I am number 17 on the list. The total reached 56 by 1982. Most people back then made the voyage as an adventurous challenge. But the BOC Challenge launched in 1982, the first solo race around the world (ignoring The Sunday Times Golden Globe), then the Vendée Globe that began later that decade changed things. The number of circumnavigators began to accelerate, largely owing to these races and reached 100 sailors by 1990.

This does not mean a circumnavigation has become simpler. The increase is rather down to an awareness of the challenge and the fact that more people are prepared to take the risks – plus better boats, better equipment and, above all, satellite communications. It is the latter that has taken away some of the risks faced in earlier age when communication was limited to single sideband radio of low power which frequently failed to connect at all. Now, if a sailor is in trouble they need only press a button and the world is alerted.

The advantage of a properly organised race is that it provides a safety structure. These days the organisers can tell exactly where the boats are at any moment via satellite tracking. It's a far cry from the earlier days when a sailor disappeared into the blue and the only news came on arrival in port or a sighting by another vessel at sea. But there are still people who want to just take off on their own. These are the real heirs of the early adventurers who sailed for personal satisfaction not fame or money.

It is interesting that despite all the modern innovations and the developments in boats, sails and rigging in the past 30 years, only about half the people who begin a round the world race make it to the finish. The figure for the last Vendée is 55 per cent, which is higher than the previous race. Since these raceboats tend to have good budgets and are sailed by professionals, you would think there could be no excuse for failing to complete the voyage. But rather than see this as a failure on the part of the pros, it is better understood as a measure of how tough this challenge really is.

And before you consider that 200 is a lot of people to have completed a proper circumnavigation, reflect on the fact that more than 600 astronauts have been into space.

SYDNEY HOBART RACE

I tick off another box in a lifetime of great racing achievements, taking part in the 2010 Rolex Sydney to Hobart Race. It didn't turn out quite as I had expected...

The Rolex Sydney to Hobart Race, established by Captain John Illingworth in 1945, is one of the great bluewater classic yacht races. The distance of 628 miles makes it remarkably similar to the Fastnet and it can be just as testing. Recent years have been rather easy and the record has dropped below two days as the modern, long, light sledges have been able to reach at high speeds nearly all the way.

But 2010 turned out to be more like a proper Sydney Hobart with some gale-force winds on the nose to slow the sledges and allow the smaller and heavier boats a chance of good handicap results.

The Cruising Yacht Club of Australia has a pleasant clubhouse and marina in Rushcutters Bay on Sydney Harbour and this is where the competing yachts gathered. We were on Richard Dobb's Swan 68 *Titania of Cowes*, a heavy cruiser-racer, and we had 19 crew. There is something to be said for yacht racing with teak decks and a cook!

Our crew were a mix of Brits, Aussies and Americans, but this provided no cultural problems. The main differences seemed to focus around my solo habit of cleating a spinnaker and sailing to its luff and Andy Green's determination to trim for every small angle of change. This cultural divide was not something that could be bridged easily in a matter of three short days!

The race traditionally starts on Boxing Day inside the harbour and then out through the heads, attracting a very large spectator fleet and plenty of people shoreside. There were 82 boats in the fleet and this number calls for two start lines, the difference being adjusted by separate buoys to be rounded as you clear the harbour.

A light north-easterly got the light boats away down the New South Wales coast, but then a front came through and we were beating into rising headwinds. That suited us, and our handicap position started to rise encouragingly. The seas were short and steep in the Force 8 winds, but we had the weight to push through them at between eight and nine knots.

Then disaster for our hopes struck when a deck-mounted liferaft washed overboard. The rules of the race are sensible and clear. You have to report before you start crossing the Bass Strait that all your safety equipment is on board and working. This we could no longer do, so we diverted to Eden and dropped off the crew who were in excess of the remaining liferaft capacity. We found three retiring boats already there and a further 16 retired over the next few hours, roughly 25 per cent of the fleet.

As we headed back out to sea the wind was easing and the Bass Strait did not provide the seriously nasty conditions that had caused casualties in earlier races. Then the wind went light and any hope we might have had of regaining our single figure handicap position drifted away.

But down the eastern Tasmanian coast the tactics are fascinating. We were told there had been only one sea breeze this year, and even allowing for some exaggeration, close inshore did not seem the right place to be, so we stayed a bit off the coast anxiously watching the boats in front and behind to see whether they had better winds inshore or offshore.

In the end it did not seem to make much difference, but we were buoyed by the cricket news that England had thrashed Australia in the 4th test and would retain the Ashes.

On the south coast we beat round the iconic cliffs off Cape Raol, which remind one of the Giant's Causeway in Ulster. Then there is a 40-mile sail up the River Derwent to the finish in Hobart's enormous harbour. Robert Oatley's 100-footer *Wild Oats* was the line honours winner, but the IRC winner was the 51-footer *Secret Men's Business*. We finished 19th on handicap, but at least we knew where we had lost out.

Hobart gives a tremendous reception to all the boats and was alive with sailors and spectators as most boats stayed on to see in the New Year there, which creates a massive party with a lovely atmosphere. I had always wanted to sail this race, so that's another box now ticked, but I would not rule out a return in the future as my trip Down Under was good fun.

CHINA SEA RACE

What chance does the former Eighties flyer *Pyewacket* have against shorter hotshot TP52s in flukey winds? Almost none as it turns out, but winning isn't all in the China Sea Race.

The biennial China Sea Race from Hong Kong to Subic Bay in the Philippines is run by one of the most enjoyable and social of the yacht clubs I know, the Royal Hong Kong. So, the invitation I received to join some friends this year was more than welcome.

At the grand old age of 23, our boat was certainly venerable. She was renowned in her time as Roy Disney's *Pyewacket,* but she had seen better days and at 70ft had a horrendous IRC handicap.

I flew to Hong Kong a few days early to get to know the boat and her crew. At 16-strong, the latter was large, but most members were old friends. We worked up, got to know our way around the boat and practised a few man-overboards just to remind people of the importance of clipping on.

Hong Kong Harbour is an exciting place to sail. The Royal Hong Kong club basin leads straight onto Victoria Harbour, where there is always plenty of bustling commercial traffic, albeit traffic of the disciplined and predictable kind.

A government land reclamation scheme will reduce the number of moorings at the club. That's not a huge problem because it sails from other locations, but I think a club loses something of itself when its activities are split. Hopefully, the club will remain its boisterous and welcoming self and continue to liven up the waters of the harbour.

The distance from Hong Kong to Subic Bay is 565 miles and the race always takes place at Easter, when the north-east monsoon begins to fade. This usually means a shy reach across the South China Sea, but once close to the island of Luzon the weather changes and becomes light.

At that point, it's decision time: stay up and take the north-easterlies as they come through or drop down and rely on being able to harden up nearer the finish where the winds are lighter. This is where a certain amount of luck comes into the equation and these races are won or lost. The wind shadow from the mountains can be very pronounced, calms are normal and the question is how to find what little wind is on offer.

So, the gamble is whether to close the shore and rely upon the land / sea breeze or to stay offshore and hope some wind exists. Then closer to the destination, a wind with more south in it is often found; south-east means a beat, south-west or even west means a reach or run – and a run in light winds is neither fast nor much fun.

You certainly wouldn't want to do this race without a wind-seeker.

There was a good field of entries this year, with 30 yachts on the start sheet. The big question for us was whether our boat could hold off the shorter, but much more modern, TP25s.

The answer was not long in coming. Our keel was small and beating out from an exciting start in Victoria Harbour off the yacht club, we pointed lower and were soon dropped by the newer boats, which not only pointed higher, but also footed faster – one of the most depressing situations in which to find oneself on the race course.

Never mind, we thought. Once we get clear and onto the rhumb line our waterline length will pay dividends. Fat chance. After losing the other boats in the mist, we went for speed, our only chance, and dropped below the rhumb line. We were the first to pick up a predicted southerly, but any fresh hope was dashed at the first reporting schedule.

We had hoped to ride this wind above the rhumb line, but it faded and we had calms while those further north of us got the new north-easterly wind before us, an advantage worth more than 20 miles. Thereafter, our distance from the others varied, but Neil Pryde's *Hi-Fi* remorselessly extended her lead over the fleet, only challenged by the first of the TPs, *Evolution Racing*.

We lay 6th on the water at the last evening schedule, but some local knowledge allowed us to call the weather right at the end. We came in to the coast, picked up the sea breeze and finished 5th over the line, less than an hour after the last TP, which was some consolation. Pryde had sailed an almost perfect race and won again, both line honours and handicap.

Still, we had a happy crew and some very enjoyable sailing, which is what it should all be about. You can't win them all.

TWO-HANDED ROUND BRITAIN RACE

It may have lost its allure in the age of gung-ho, global events but the two-handed Round British Isles Race is a uniquely tactical challenge that allows no margin for error. And that makes for exciting racing.

Every four years, a few dozen yachtsmen make a pilgrimage to many of the sea areas so familiar to listeners of the shipping forecasts. Their reason is to compete in the two-handed Round British Isles Race, organised by the Royal Western Yacht Club in Plymouth, which has been run regularly since 1966. With the sole exception of Sicily, the British Isles is the only part of Europe that can be sailed around in its entirety and the course passes outside all of the region's islets apart from Rockall and the Channel Isles.

In the Seventies the race won a lot of coverage and attracted big names but it has lost some of its media allure, in part because today's round-the-world races make sailing around Britain seem less daring. But this misunderstands what is involved in this event, which breeds a competitive but friendly spirit among contestants.

We don't have the Southern Ocean, nor giant waves and near freezing seawater. But neither do we have steady tradewinds and the sea room of an ocean to provide tactical choices if things turn nasty. The challenge of sailing round the British Isles is that there is land to starboard all the way, sometimes very close, so navigation is a constant concern and relaxation is impossible.

There are also the tactical problems of our constantly changing weather. The changes in wind strength and direction require accurate prediction then careful planning, often when very tired. The two crew, taking turns on watch, not only have to make the sail changes that the weather demands but give constant attention to the weather and the tactics it requires and ensure a reach along a distant rocky shore does not become a beat off a lee shore an hour later.

These natural obstacles make the event much tougher than an Atlantic race even though the distance may be 1,000 miles shorter. The competitive pressure is tremendous and a few hours under the wrong sail or on the wrong tack, which might have a chance of being regained in the vastness of the Atlantic, are seldom recovered in this race.

The race is in five legs: Plymouth to Cork (230 miles); Cork to Barra in the Outer Hebrides (460 miles); outside St Kilda to Muckle Flugga, the most northerly island of the British Isles, to Lerwick (420 miles); a 470-mile run down the east coast to Lowestoft; then a 305-mile leg back to the finish at Plymouth via the Dover Straits and English Channel. Contestants have 48 hours in each port; they can stay longer if they wish but if they do it counts as sailing time. The idea is to provide a chance for maintenance and rest, although the social activities provided by the host clubs in Cork, Lerwick and Lowestoft can make 48-hour stopovers as challenging as the racing.

The cliffs and islands of Ireland, the beauty and eerie stillness of Castle Bay in the Hebrides and the long days and almost non-existent nights around the northern Scottish coast leave indelible memories. Best forgotten is the bash down the North Sea usually into a south-westerly, which kicks up a nasty short wave in the shallow waters. But the Royal Norfolk and Suffolk Yacht Club's breakfast bloaters compensate even for that. The race usually intensifies for that final dash back to Plymouth and on many occasions the leader will have changed while sailing down Channel. No one dares to relax when one miscall on the tide can rob you of a place. This leads to an exciting finish but is hard on the sailor's nerves, especially when they cannot be certain of the other boats' positions.

Rumour has it that the race was set up to prove that multihulls were incapable of competing against monohulls on a challenging course with plenty of windward work. If this was the objective it was a failure. Only once, in 1970, has the race been won by a monohull (a 71-footer). This is no longer possible as the race now limits monohulls to 50ft and multis to 45ft. The minimum length for both is now 30ft.

This reduction in lengths means that previous records are less likely to be broken. But you can be sure that won't stop people from trying.

ROUND THE ISLAND RACE

An Open 60 is not the most nimble craft when boxed in by 300 other competitors around a mark. Luckily the Round the Island Race is as much about genial sportsmanship as results.

Stuck off Bembridge Ledge buoy, in the middle of at least 300 other yachts all trying to get round with zero wind – just little gasps and from different directions – is not the place for an Open 60. Of course, we shouldn't have been there. We should have been miles ahead – but we weren't. If someone had wanted to apply the racing rules there would have been chaos; you could probably have walked across a width of 300m of yachts with no more than a step between them.

Anyone trying to be clever could have caused collisions, damage and possibly injury. What impressed me was how sensible everyone was being. There was little shouting; perhaps the odd raised voice to be heard, but no notes of panic. Well there was one exception when a boat, having got a puff of wind charged into the melee and nearly hit our stern, but slick crew work by the boats around checked her before she damaged herself, us and other boats around. Eventually, a little wind got up and we were all able to escape.

It was a wonderful example of good sportsmanship and common sense. Had the wind freshened by just a couple of knots, the situation would have become more dangerous, but then, had there been a couple more knots of wind, the situation would probably not have developed in the first place.

As I said, we should have been miles ahead at this stage, but we had lost quite a lot of time when we had gone offshore into the greater adverse tide behind the Island. The problem with an Open 60 is that its mainsail has a huge roach, so the rig is like most multihulls – there is no fixed backstay, the mast is supported aft by runners.

They are designed for the empty oceans and not short-tacking, so we cannot crash-tack or gybe quickly and it pays to keep clear of other boats that might have right of way.

The incident occurred in this year's Island Sailing Club's Round the Island Race sponsored by JP Morgan Asset Management. The wind was not strong enough for a threat to the record and there were some frustrating calm patches, but everyone experienced them at some time or another.

The race has been described as sailing's favourite event and with some justification. After the London Marathon and the Great North Run, this is the biggest participation event in British sport. No doubt someone will know how many crew were involved, but a guess was made at 14,000, which does not seem unreasonable.

This year there were 1,789 boats entered, from the mighty 98ft ICAP Leopard to small craft a sixth of her length; from yachts with crews of 20 or more to those with just two. It is that cross-section of sailing which makes the event so special. This is an event where a family can enter their boat and enjoy the excitement and achievement among so many fellow sailors. The casual cruiser-racers in the same event as the hotshots.

A key element of the event's universal appeal is that the course is so straightforward; a race round an island is as simple to set out as it is for everyone to follow. Bembridge is the only mark of the course that has to be passed by everyone because the Queen's Harbour Master in Portsmouth wanted the Spitsand Fort to be optional to keep some boats clear of the channel.

The fact that this benefits the smaller boats by a considerable amount is not necessarily a cause for complaint from a racing point of view, but it is a pity. It creates a form of handicap which did not exist before. The leg from the forts to the finish line off Cowes is usually a beat and against the tide, so the shallower the water, the less adverse the tide, plus there is usually a slight wind benefit close to the Island shore.

The larger boats cannot sensibly go south of the fort without a serious risk of grounding, so once they have passed north of it they have to tack along the north shore to gain similar benefits of tidal avoidance, but without the usually freer wind. Still, the big boats tend to race against each other, so this does not affect their class, only their overall position.

At the end of the day, a Folkboat was the overall winner this year and another Folkboat 2nd, which brought smiles to nearly all faces.

COWES-TORBAY-COWES RACE

I have sailed from Cowes to Torbay numerous times during my decades of sailing around the South Coast, but this was the first passage on which I clocked 50 knots on the log.

I had never been in a powerboat race before, so when Shelley Jory, Britain's ladies' powerboat champion, asked if I would care to navigate for her in the Cowes-Torbay-Cowes powerboat classic I was intrigued. I thought it might be interesting to see how the other half of boating went about its sport and what the boats were like.

We were entered in the cruiser class. That is a relative term as the top speed of our Scorpion RIB, weighing in at 3 tons and with twin diesels developing 630hp between them, was 53 knots.

The start was not what I expected. No guns at ten, four, then one minute, nor any fixed line. The fleet of 20 boats lined up abreast and kept pace with a Red Funnel fast ferry at 34 knots until the starter decided that we were in line and up went a green flag. Instantly we were at full throttle, crashing along in the calm waters of the Solent.

A small RIB in our path stopped and its driver held up his hands in surrender. A sailing yacht crossing the western Solent getting in the way, had a rude shock as the powerboats roared past. It looked impressive – it certainly felt impressive – even if we were quickly left behind by monsters with up to 2,000hp.

As we approached Hurst the first casualty came into view. We closed to see if they needed assistance, but it was an engine problem and there were plenty of race official boats around. The waves grew, our motion became more violent. On our boat we had rests instead of seats, so it paid to keep your legs slightly bent to absorb the shock when we crashed down on a wave every couple of seconds. We were being thrown about violently – it was as bad as a knockdown.

Looking ahead over the windscreen gave some warning, but I was beginning to wonder why I had signed up for four hours-plus of this punishment. We passed more casualties, but our engines were roaring nicely, making conversation without our intercom totally impossible. As it happened a chat was not foremost on my mind because the navigation became interesting. My years spent racing in this stretch of water now came in handy. Most of the boats were heading straight along the rhumb line for Portland Bill, but the waves were quite big, with a Force 5 having built up the sea. As all Solent sailors know, wind against tide off the St Albans can be quite unpleasant.

We steered an initial course inside Anvil, coming into calmer water as we approached Swanage and then around the corner, keeping close to the shore, where the waves were smaller. Somewhere about Lulworth we steered out for Portland Bill, the waves noticeably lower, so our speed higher. At Portland we had overtaken three of the more powerful boats which had been forced to slow by the bigger waves offshore.

From Portland to Torbay the coastal route adds about eight miles – or around 20 per cent – to the total distance. Our speed, even in the quite large waves was still over 40 knots, not enough to hold the big beasts, but mathematically better, and about halfway across the Lyme Bay the waves began to shrink and speed improved.

Torbay was calm and we swept around the two marks at 50-plus knots, being overtaken by a much faster RIB that had gone inshore and should not have been behind us. Returning the rhumb line made sense back to Portland and we were running at close to 50 knots for half the distance, slowing as the waves became bigger. When you are travelling at these speeds, it is only slightly easier to be powering over a following sea, so as we lost the lee our speed dropped.

Perhaps the most uncomfortable part was crossing Poole Bay and I was relieved when we rounded Hurst for the last sprint to the finish near Egypt Point. As we closed the finish, our friend from Torbay closed in on us again, but he had left it too late and finished a minute behind us.

We finished 4th out of nine finishers, but won the cruiser class. We had a very aggressive driver in Shelley and I enjoyed the navigation and the friendliness of the other racers. Even though two weeks later I still carried bruises from the contact with the boat, when pressed I said would be back next year for the 50th anniversary – but as a spectator. I shall stick to sails.

WINTER RACE ON THE THAMES

Winter sailing is the antidote to crowded summer anchorages and the Thames Frostbite Race provides a spot of convivial competition.

The winter months have traditionally been when we haul out our boats, clean off the accumulated weed and barnacles, and carry out repairs. Sometimes we even get round to making those small improvements we have talked about, but never quite got around to all season.

But apart from the need to apply new antifouling and tidy up, why do we lose the whole of winter? We all know how busy and crowded our favourite anchorages become during summer. Newtown Creek on the Isle of Wight is an obvious example, but there are plenty more.

In winter months these popular anchorages are usually empty. And there is something magical about climbing up on deck on a still, frosty or misty morning, the first mug of tea in hand, and surveying a quiet anchorage that you have to yourself or else share with friends' yachts after a cruise in company.

Not that all mornings are frosty or misty, of course. We get periods of quite pleasant conditions in which to sail if we have kept our boats on their mooring and available to take out.

In February 1976, with *Suhaili* moored in St Katharine Docks, a conversation in the clubhouse led to the organisation of the Thames Frostbite Race. Twenty-seven boats started at Tower Bridge just as the ebb commenced and sailed downriver to Erith for a convivial evening with the Erith Yacht Club, housed in those days on an old car ferry. The next day we raced back to St Katharine's with the flood tide. Anyone who has sailed the Thames will appreciate that to have raced against the tide was not a clever option!

The fleet was mixed. It consisted mainly of cruisers, but someone turned up in a Flying Fifteen. Our rudimentary handicap system proved inadequate for dealing with her, so a special arbitrary factor had to be added to the calculations. The race has been repeated a number of times since, achieving 56 entries at its peak. There is much less traffic on the Thames now, so the empty expanses of river are interesting to sail if you are prepared to pull to the side if a vessel arrives. While the tides tend to dictate passages up and down the river, there are some good anchorages.

There are few options to drop the hook in the upper part of the river west from the Royal Docks – the bottom used to be hard gravel and an anchor rarely held. Gone are the days when Thames barges were moored everywhere as handy 'wharves' to wait for a favourable tide, and the wash from river-buses up here can make a berth uncomfortable.

But below the Royal Docks where the river widens, no longer confined by walls and sheet piling, there are more options; places such as Erith, Greenhithe and Thurrock where the barges used to lie. There are still marshes on the south side below Erith, but land with care as the banks are thick cloying mud.

To encourage more sailing activity to the river four Thames-based yacht clubs have united to revive the Frostbite Race and turn it into an annual event, this year to be held over the weekend of the 23-24 February. Nor is it just an individual race – there's also a prize for the most successful club in the overall results.

By including the Little Ship Club, based near Southwark Bridge, and Thurrock Yacht Club just up from Tilbury via the Greenwich and Erith yacht clubs, the clubs represent most sailors on the river. St Katharine Docks have offered a special rate for boats visiting for the event, so other club members nearby can join in and bring some leisure life to the river.

Those who have never sailed the Thames might find it a good excuse to see London from a different angle. The formula for the Frostbite is the same: a two-stage race over two days, all sailed with the tides. Come and join in – the event will provide an opportunity for those who keep their boats afloat over the winter to enjoy a mildly competitive, but convivial weekend. It is what club sailing should be all about.

PLACES

"There are some ports that always leave a lifelong impression."

Robin Knox-Johnston, March 2006

SOUTHERN OCEAN

Never mind Cape Horn at the end, a non-stop procession of cold fronts and squalls keeps us on our toes in the Southern Ocean.

The Southern Ocean is a cold, windy, miserable place. If it were like any other ocean it would probably have more yachts sailing it, but it isn't and it hasn't.

The succession of low pressure systems and fronts during a Southern Ocean summer are like the weather we get in winter in the UK. And that is its peculiar attraction. It is such a thoroughly unpleasant and demanding place to sail that it provides the ultimate challenge to a yachtsman. No one in their right mind sails down there in winter. There's a very good reason why the season for round-the-world races is the Southern Hemisphere summer.

Cold fronts and depressions passing east are the reason for this fearsome reputation. Tactically, sailing east – running your easting down, as it used to be called – you keep north of the depressions but you cannot avoid the fronts. The barometer falls, you see a long line of dark cumulus coming towards you and prepare.

Beneath or just before the cloud reaches you, the wind rises by ten or more knots, then it eases back again once the cloud is overhead. Then the wind might veer or this might just be one of a number of line squalls passing through ahead of the front and there is no change in wind direction.

You don't know and have to assume this might be the actual front and be ready. Sometimes this can last several hours which is tiring, especially if you are solo and need to be on standby to reef for the real thing.

Once the real front has passed and the wind starts to ease, you need to keep power up, so more sail has to be set. If you don't keep moving, the waves take charge and the boat gets thrown around a lot; uncomfortable at best, an involuntary gybe at worst.

It's also less bumpy if you keep moving. I could let *Suhaili* bounce around with warps out – she wasn't going to come to any harm – but these light machines need to be driven.

However, the wind and rain squalls are probably still there, the weather going calm and veering as much as 60° as they approach. If you're lucky, your autopilot can be set to steer a course by the wind angle, which at least allows a little rest occasionally and avoids the risk of an unwanted gybe. There is as much sail handling here as in the Doldrums but the winds are much more ferocious. You can see why square-riggers were able to make this journey, gybing was not a problem for them, just a slight adjustment to sheets and guys, whereas a yacht has to pull everything from one side to the other. And on Open 60s and multihulls that means the backstays too – and that's one piece of rigging you must get right.

The seawater temperatures are about the same as for the Northern Hemisphere, but for a latitude 10° further from the Pole. Ice was sighted off New Zealand this year at about the same distance from the Equator as northern France. The southerly winds are the cold ones as they come from Antarctica. This is when the squalls produce hail or snow instead of rain. You don't want cuts on your hands when the hail is about.

And at the end of it all there is Cape Horn. You breathe a huge sigh of relief when that bears west but first you have to get around it. The Southern Ocean narrows from 2,000 miles to 600 and the Andes concentrate the winds through the gap as the ocean bottom rises. The result can be even stronger winds and steeper seas in this area. Nor are the winds always westerly – a surprisingly high proportion are easterlies. We had an easterly gale when we rounded an ENZA a few years ago.

There is an association for those who have rounded Cape Horn under sail. But Cape Horn is just the climax. All members have experienced the Southern Ocean just to get there and membership holds the same cachet now as when it was the prerogative of the square-rig seamen. You have taken on the worst and seen Nature in its rawest state to qualify.

CAPE HORN

A Force 7, whisky and aunty's fruit cake marked a wet ride around Cape Horn. It also proved straightforward compared with a nerve-racking beat up the Beagle Channel.

It was my third rounding of Cape Horn and, being realistic, it is probably my last. I don't like closing doors, I like to keep my options open, but I cannot see what opportunity might arise to allow me another rounding. It made me a little sad, but this is not a place you want to hang around and the relief when it bears west is huge.

As with *Suhaili* 38 years before, I made a landfall on the Diego Ramirez group, which gives a safe offing. The wind was Force 7 from the south-south-west and if it had backed, it would have been a hard beat to get round, so searoom seemed sensible.

In fact, the wind did back, but I was able to clear the Cape by eight miles, a safe margin. I toasted it with whisky and opened the fruit cake my 100-year-old aunt had made for me, just as she had 38 years before. The swell was huge and the waves aggressive, so it was a wet rounding and the Cape itself was frequently hidden by dark rain squalls, which added to the atmosphere.

It was easy to imagine what an awful place this must have been to the seamen on the square-riggers and why the Cape is considered the Everest of the seas. I saw the two horns of rock that stick out to the south, but the name was given to the Cape by the Dutchman Schouton, who named it after Hoorn in the Netherlands, I believe. It was anglicised to Horn.

Normally, I would have headed on east or north-east to the Le Maire Strait, but I had decided to pull in from the Velux 5-Oceans race to obtain a new mainsail headboard car and, while I was at it, try to get my two non-functioning satellite systems fixed. So once round, I headed nearly north to Chilean-owned Nuevo Island, which marks the southern entrance to the Beagle Channel. My objective, Ushuaia, was not the ideal choice. Port Stanley in the Falklands would have been simpler – a lot simpler as I was to discover – but there is only one flight a week from the UK to Port Stanley and the times did not work. It meant accepting a 48-hour penalty stop, but this seemed reasonable in exchange for being able to download weather information, which I had lacked for four weeks and was hampering my tactics.

It was blowing a gale as I rounded Nuevo Island which marks the southern end of the channel, and I turned west for a hard beat in a very lumpy sea, with dark rain clouds every 20 minutes or so and higher gusts of wind. On the Raymarine plotter I soon realised we were making too much leeway, so I held my breath and hardened the mainsail. I just had to hope the sliders would stay attached because, unless I powered up, we were going to end up having to make a very difficult tack in a high, but short sea – probably impossible, a wear round was more likely, or be pushed onto the Argentine coast to the north. In the gloom, spray and rain, we slammed way north of west as close to the wind as I could. Whoever decided that hell had to be hot?

Another problem was kelp. The ideal boat for the Beagle should have a long keel or be a fin keel with a skeg to avoid catching on kelp. Saga Insurance is a magnet for the stuff.

I had a rendezvous with a tow boat off Picton Island, but had to get there first as there was no way they could have passed a tow line in those conditions. Then I got 20° freer for 30 minutes and that gave me the space I needed. I headed up towards Picton, but at that moment their Iridium phone ran out of power and my VHF has a very limited range, so we lost contact.

I was now making ten knots up an unknown channel, with no idea what to expect except that I would have to turn west at the top and that would mean short tacks, or I could bale out and head back out to sea. If stress is meant to be good for you, I was getting a lot of goodness!

Then a light appeared to port. I could not make it out, but it appeared to be keeping pace. It came closer and, to my immense relief, identified itself as my tow. Now all we had to do was get a line across, but they guided me close into the land where the wind suddenly dropped away entirely and we were able to take on crew and line. I have seldom felt so relieved. You can soon tell if people know what they are doing and Jonathon Selby and Alex were obviously competent, so once we were under tow we had a stiff whisky and I turned in, my first rest for 40 hours.

We arrived in Ushuaia at daybreak and moored up with some difficulty as the wind was gusting nicely. Ushuaia is backed by mountains and snow had fallen during the night. It looked lovely. The town itself is still expanding, but there was no time for sightseeing. Simon Clay had arrived with the spares and we set to work, assisted by the crew of the yacht Zephyrus. By Tuesday all systems were functioning so not wishing to lose time or daylight, I cast off for the 60-mile passage down the Beagle Channel and back to the open sea again.

The channel is bound by high mountains on either side, so the wind funnels down it. This is not a place to be single-handed. The wind was 10-33 knots from the south-south-west, which made some of the passages where we had to turn south-east interesting, but the scenery was breathtaking – Argentina to the north, Chile to the south and in places the channel narrows to under a mile.

I progressed eastwards and it was becoming dark as I approached Picton Island again, but here the channel widens and life became easier. I reached Nuevo Island 11 hours from Ushuaia. It was a relief to be clear and, if I ever come here again, it will be in a stout cruiser with a powerful engine and a good crew.

Now the decision had to be made whether to go inside Staten Island or sail further east and round it. The tides for the Le Maire Strait between the island and Tierra del Fuego looked neutral, they are pretty strong and set up overfalls, but I went for the Strait, which I have never seen before. The sea started to flatten once within it and coming out on the north side was like coming into a totally different climate. The dark clouds receded and for the first time for a month there was not that huge rolling Southern Ocean swell. With a wind north of west, we headed off at 11 knots for the south-east corner of the Falkland Islands. I was clear of the Southern Ocean, perhaps for the last time – but who knows?

NORTH-WEST AND NORTH-EAST PASSAGES

A short cut to the Pacific via the North-west and North-east passages may become commonplace if Arctic ice continues to melt, and the implications for yachtsmen are profound.

Much publicity has been given to two German merchant vessels that traversed the North East Passage, east to west, last August and September. By taking this route rather than the Suez Canal, the distance between Korea and Europe was reduced by 3,000 miles and the time taken by nine days to 23 days.

It sounds good. We can all understand the benefits of faster shipment times and lower fuel requirements. However, these are not the first vessels to have traversed the passage. The Swede Nils Nordeskold was the first to make the passage in 1879, completed after he was iced up for the winter in the steamship *Vega*, and the first trip with icebreakers was made in 1915. And an infamous passage was made in 1940 by the German Auxiliary commerce raider *Komet*, which preyed on Allied shipping until sunk by British boats.

But the route has been used fairly frequently in recent years, with the assistance of Soviet ice-breakers. The significance of this latest transit was that ice-breakers barely had to be used.

Scientists have watched the Arctic ice cap dwindle in recent decades, not just covering a smaller area, but dramatically diminishing in thickness. This happens to coincide with the North West Passage also being open, the first occasion that the North East and North West Passages have been open simultaneously, and if global warming continues, these routes are likely to become more frequently used in summer.

There are two ways of looking at this development. On one hand, the challenge of getting through either passage has been diminished. But the thinning of the ice, if it continues at its present rate, will eventually open up many thousands of miles of coastline that was not accessible to small cruising boats. Initially at least, there is going to be the opportunity to explore shorelines that have not been ice-free since before the first boats were floated. This is a mouth-watering opportunity, something akin to the great age of exploration of the Earth which finished several hundred years ago.

In recent years a number of people have managed to get through the North West Passage in small boats – David Scott Cowper comes instantly to mind – but we can expect to see many more making the voyage now that it has become much more clear and achievable.

The opening of the Arctic could cause some changes to round the world racing. We shall have to redefine a circumnavigation. Until now, with neither of the passages open, it has always been taken to mean a voyage from the Northern Hemisphere south around the three great capes of Good Hope, Leeuwin and the Horn and back to the starting point.

For those sailing from the Southern Hemisphere, the World Sailing Speed Record Committee (WSSRC) decided it was necessary to sail into the Northern and round an obvious point, such as the Azores, so that the voyage exceeded 21,600 nautical miles, the WSSRC's current standard. If more ice melts it is going to become possible to leave Northern Europe and circumnavigate the world without crossing south of the Equator for the first time.

One can envisage record attempts for this voyage, perhaps a summer race developing, but will this count as a proper circumnavigation? To comply with the existing rule any future voyage around the Arctic ice cap (if it continues to exist) would have to include a dive south across the Equator at some stage around a clearly defined point, so the total distance exceeds 21,600 nautical miles before the sailor could be considered. But if the Arctic becomes ice-free – and ice thickness has halved in the past 40 years – we may soon take a route to the Pacific Ocean via the North Pole.

Whether we dive into the Southern Hemisphere or not, we shall need to decide which great Arctic capes must be left to the south.

What may be far more alarming as the ice disappears is the thought of the wind blowing around the world uninterrupted by land in the northern latitudes, just as it can do in the Southern Ocean, and building up the huge waves we experience in the Southern Hemisphere.

DURBAN

As yachtsmen, there are always places that leave a special imprint on your heart. One such port is Durban in South Africa.

There are some ports that always leave a lifelong impression, and, for me, one of these is Durban in South Africa. I called there during my Merchant Navy days, but never really got to know it – just another port really. But when we called in while sailing *Suhaili* back from India in 1966, it was a very different matter.

The month was April, the beginning of winter in the Southern Hemisphere and we had some maintenance to do, but more importantly, we needed to top up the treasury in order to find food for the next leg to Cape Town.

Durban was, and is, Africa's busiest port and so priority is rightly given to commercial traffic. In those days, before VHF was common, you had to wait for a pilot to take you in, the pilot vessel being larger than we were! The pilots were most helpful though and were able to pass on a great deal of useful information as they conned us through the harbour to the yacht moorings.

We berthed at the Royal Natal Yacht Club, adjacent to the Point YC which gave automatic temporary membership to crews of visiting yachts. This was something we had grown accustomed to on our way down the coast of Africa, and it gave us a bit of a shock when we got back to the UK and found this was very far from the norm.

The club members quickly found us jobs. I went as Master of a coaster until jaundice forced me ashore, after which I took up stevedoring. When we had free time we hauled *Suhaili* out of the water and quietly got on with the inevitable long list of jobs. When back in the water we naturally joined in the club's functions, a particularly nice tradition being the beginning of the season sail past, where every boat in commission sailed round the bay in a set order and then past the commodore, cheering as they did so. The poor commodore had to reciprocate the cheers so he was left speechless for a week!

The jetty collected all the visiting yachts and while we were there, *Sandefjord*, an original Colin Archer, was brought in by the Cullen brothers after a circumnavigation. Bruce Dalling, later to come 2nd in the 1968 OSTAR, arrived from Hong Kong in his Vertue and Dr David Lewis, veteran of the first OSTAR, arrived in *Rehu Moana* on a circumnavigation with his two small girls as crew.

The latter went aground on the sandbank when he arrived during the night and we went out and towed him in, enabling us to meet someone whose achievements inspired admiration.

The yacht jetty was a very social place to be and *Sandefjord*, as the largest boat, was the venue for some pleasant parties. Before we left, the number of visitors had swelled to a dozen yachts so even *Sandefjord* began to feel small, but summer was coming and most of us had left by November.

Visiting with the Clipper fleet at the end of last year, we received the same warm welcome. The old wooden jetty had gone and that corner of the harbour and the approach channel had been dredged to more than three metres and new pontoons installed to take our fleet of 68-footers. The city has decided that yachting is an asset to its reputation as South Africa's playground and is going to invest.

Forty years ago *Suhaili* was, at 32ft, an average-sized yacht, but a lot has happened in the meantime and the average globe-girdling cruiser is larger these days and needs more water. The two lines of trots have become four, the sandbank having been dredged to provide the extra deep water. Two of them are fitted with pontoons which doubles the numbers in the same space, so there were probably three times as many yachts moored there. The Royal Natal has moved into a new building alongside the marina so the two clubs nestle close to each other.

Wednesday evening races are attracting fleets of up to 50 yachts, sailing round the harbour but being prepared to live with the occasional moving mark of an incoming or departing merchant ship, which have to be avoided.

People who cruise round the world quickly learn from others where the friendly ports are that can provide a stopover to rest, make repairs, restock, and enjoy a pleasant environment. My retirement cruise will definitely include Durban.

BOMBAY

I return to Bombay, where *Suhaili* was built, and remember the pleasures of sailing from the Royal Bombay Yacht Club 40 years ago.

There is nothing so self-indulgent as wandering down Memory Lane, and a recent visit to Bombay provided the perfect opportunity. Sadly, the Bundar where we built *Suhaili* has been replaced by a long ferry pier but, apart from some more tall buildings, not much had appreciably changed around the centre of the city.

The view of the Gateway to India from Bombay harbour, with the imposing structure of the Taj Mahal Hotel, is familiar to most people, but how many recognise the large colonial building to its immediate right?

This was, and still is, the home of the Royal Bombay Yacht Club. Founded in 1846, it received its Royal charter in 1876, and, like the Royal Hong Kong Yacht Club, has kept the 'royal' in its title. It proudly occupies one of the finest sites in the city.

Forty years ago, when my ship was in Bombay each month, we used to go and sail their Seabird class dinghies from the Gateway of India steps. I seem to remember it cost about £2 for a day, and that included the Tindal who tended the boat and always came as one of the crew as Sahibs could not be trusted with his boat without him! These boatmen were invaluable as they knew the harbour inside out and had an uncanny aptitude for reading the wind.

If there were enough of us, we could man two boats and race – Elephanta Island, with its incredible caves, was one destination, or a mark to round in the annual race for the Duke of Edinburgh's Cup. Alternatively, right across the harbour at Mandwa, then deserted but now a very smart suburb of an ever-expanding city, the club kept a small pavilion which was a pleasant spot for a picnic.

Another interesting cruise was up the harbour to the country craft anchorage and the site there had not changed in centuries. These traditional trading vessels were built along similar lines to dhows, but with a lower freeboard, and there used to be hundreds of them anchored just upriver from the main port, not far from where we built *Suhaili*. They sailed along the Indian coast using only a lateen sail for power, no engine and many had no deck – no different from a Viking Gnarr.

Tying alongside one of these craft to chat with the crew was always fascinating as they served the creeks and small ports that large vessels could not reach, a tantalising cruising prospect. It was from these crews that I learnt of their simple trick to patch up a leak in the planking to hold until they next hauled ashore for refit and proper recaulking.

They took a baler, tied it to a long bamboo pole, filled it with cement, and then lowered it into the water until it was close to the leak. Then they shook the pole so the cement would be washed out of the baler into the water and sucked into the leak. They would probably have been better using shavings or sawdust, but that was their method.

Arab dhows were still to be seen in reasonable numbers bringing cargoes like dates from the Shatt-al-Arab. Most had the canoe stern we associate with this type of craft, but quite a number had the transom stern copied from the European galleons. Their trades took them all over the Indian Ocean under sail, and you would see more than 200 moored up at Basra when the date harvest was being shipped out.

In the season we used to load up to a couple of thousand tons of dates, wrapped in palm baskets, and the contents of the bilges were much prized when we got back to Bombay, going to produce an illegal form of arak, known colloquially as *daru* (gunpowder) which cost 1/6d a pint, but no one in their right senses drank it without very heavy dilution.

Forty years ago there was prohibition in Bombay, and a Customs Officer sat in at every bar selling alcohol, marking your permit every time you bought a drink until your ration was finished for that month. Now, a more relaxed regime exists and the Royal Bombay Yacht Club bar is a very sociable place to visit. The Seabirds are still in use, venerable old ladies now, but lovingly cared for, but the club now has a strong fleet of Lasers and sailing is much more active.

If anyone is thinking of cruising out East, I cannot think of a more pleasant watering hole.

INDIAN OCEAN

Once it was only desperate fishermen who launched from shore. Now Indian Ocean piracy sees ruthless mercenaries sail from motherships in an industry worth billions – and that has implications for us all.

The northern Indian Ocean is becoming a no-go area for yachts as the piratical activity off Somalia spreads and protection for sailors remains limited. Attacks have now taken place north of Aden in the Red Sea, as far south as the Seychelles and as far east as the Maldives. The waters around Oman in the Indian Ocean are also vulnerable.

The international naval presence has become more effective near the Somalian coast, but this has only forced the pirates to sail further afield, hugely expanding the area of risk. Perhaps more worrying is that the pirates have changed their tactics. Rather than run fast sorties from shore, they now use captured vessels as motherships, their crews still aboard as hostages, thereby extending their range of operation.

At present, 23 vessels with as many as 600 hostages are being held for ransom. This has become a multi-billion pound problem that affects us all. It restricts our cruising grounds, of course. But in addition, we all suffer from the hike in insurance for cargo vessels to cover the risk to life and property.

Naval escorts are hamstrung because governments will not unite to find a common solution to the problem, and concerns about the human rights of the pirates appear to outweigh those of innocent seafarers. It is small wonder that many ship owners now hire their own armed security when their boats traverse these waters.

The problem for navies is that these pirates can strike almost anywhere and without warning. It is very hard for the warships to deal with this because once the pirates are aboard a vessel the crew are at risk if any action is taken. The Russian crew of one vessel managed to immobilise their engines and lock themselves away from harm, thereby allowing marines to board and deal with the pirates. Those that survived are now facing a long sojourn in Siberia. But few cargo vessels are built with a 'citadel' in which the crew can lock themselves away and await rescue. Yachts, meanwhile, are completely vulnerable.

The danger level is increasing too. The original pirates were fishermen who had been forced to desperate measures as foreign vessels depleted their livelihoods, and they treated prisoners relatively well. But as the awareness of piracy as a profitable enterprise has grown, it has drawn in former soldiers who are backed by ever more sophisticated organisations. And their attitudes towards life are far more ruthless.

The murder of four Americans during a rescue attempt this February and the capture of a Danish family a month later have emphasised just how vulnerable yachts are. Yachting families are not a primary target; they are not profitable hostages as they occupy their captors' time for a limited reward, as was shown by the Chandlers. But if the merchant vessels become harder targets, yachts might suddenly become more attractive.

Advice on how yachts should transit the Indian Ocean varies. It has been suggested that shooting at approaching pirate craft will persuade pirates to seek an easier target, but this is a high-risk strategy. Leaving aside that it assumes the pirate craft is recognisable as such when it comes within range, it ignores the fact that many pirates are now heavily armed. Potshots could only provoke.

Turning away from an approaching threat can work as the pirate craft have a limited range and don't like to stray too far from their motherships. But this means you have to be able to outrun them – unlikely for a yacht. Convoys are another option but only if they have a naval escort to frighten away potential attackers. Tying down expensive, sophisticated warships to escort a slow-moving convoy is not the best use of an asset whose primary purpose is to protect international trade.

So what's the answer? At present there is only one – avoid the Indian Ocean entirely until piracy has been eliminated. This seems unlikely while there is no effective government in Somalia to take control of the problem.

It seems sad that the wonderful waters of east Africa are no longer safe sailing grounds, but it is surely better to accept this as fact rather than spend a year in captivity and face bankruptcy to buy your freedom.

Just as sad is that vessels will no longer have the Mediterranean, Red Sea and Indian Ocean to explore on a slow circumnavigation. For the foreseeable future the only safe route to and from Asia and Australia from Europe is round the Cape of Good Hope or through the Panama Canal.

GREENLAND

You can never be sure, when you set off for the far north, whether the ice will let you reach your destination and this summer the ice was unusually heavy.

Ever since 1991 when Chris Bonington and I tried to get to the summit of Cathedral Mountain in Greenland but found we had climbed the neighbouring and lesser peak, we have talked about going back. This year we checked our diaries and set off from Iceland, climbing and ski equipment loaded aboard *Antiope*.

The 60-footer had been cruising Icelandic waters for more than a month but had reported unseasonable weather, which was not very encouraging. Gales in midsummer are not normal; usually the lows that depart America swing round the western side of Greenland during the summer, but Iceland had received more than usual.

The ice too, seemed to be hanging around much longer along the East Greenland coast, showing a depth of 80 miles as far south as Angmassalik, when 20 would be the most to be expected on the coast in late July and much less near the entrances to fjords where the tidal flow tends to clear a lot of the ice away.

However we had made our plans, July and August are the best months, as the ice usually recedes and the weather is still benign, so we decided to head across the 300-mile wide Denmark Strait towards Kangerlussuaq Fjord and investigate for ourselves.

Mist accompanied us most of the way and knowing that radar does not receive a good echo from ice we kept a permanent lookout, fortunately helped by only a couple of hours of twilight at night, although the temperature dropped to freezing during those hours. Some light brash ice was sighted 60 miles from the coast, more or less where predicted, but this was the southern edge of a large bight focused on our objective.

Leaving it to starboard we pressed on. The mountains were now tantalisingly in sight, misleading in these latitudes where the peculiar refraction brings them into view at more than 80 miles and distances can easily be misjudged. Around 48 miles from the fjord a line of bergy bits appeared ahead so a lookout was sent to the masthead. He reported clearer water further south. It looked a mile, but was in fact five miles before the ice thinned and we followed it in. The entrance to the fjord was clearly visible, 36 miles away, and we could even see our mountain in the distance, a further 30 miles inland.

Working through ice like this, perhaps covering 50-70 per cent of the surface, is not too difficult but it is not something to be rushed. Speed has to be slow as ice is just floating rock and many of the bits have sharp underhangs. They show clearly enough in the crystal water and are not difficult to avoid, but it pays to be going slowly and have a very manoeuvrable boat.

Here and there the lookout called out a lead of less dense ice and we crept in towards these to increase our overall speed. They looked open, but there were always small bits to avoid. Hour followed hour of this, the helm being changed frequently as after a while everyone becomes a little less cautious.

After eight hours we had closed to within five miles of the fjord entrance but the ice was becoming thicker and shortly afterwards even the lookout could not see a lead. We stopped and waited for a while, as sometimes the ice will clear as bergs, some affected by wind and some by tide, seldom move at the same speed. This time, though, the ice stayed resolutely tight.

If the ice was this tight so far from the entrance we could imagine what it must be like inside the fjord. Fourteen years before we had got right through the entrance and only come across dense stuff when we reached Watkins Fjord, 14 miles inside. This ice was solid, and hanging around in ice is not very sensible so we turned about. We were not going to reach the Cathedral this year.

We cleared the ice in six hours and decided to try to get to Angmassalik, the only town on the east coast, 200 miles to the south, but quickly ran into ice much further out to sea than predicted. Indeed, we were still dodging ice 100 miles off the coast. Then a low was forecast, coming up the east coast giving gale force winds that would give a lee of ice. This was no place to be so we reluctantly headed back to Iceland.

LES SABLES-D'OLONNE

They do things differently in France, where sailors are seen as gladiators and millions come to watch the start of a race. Maybe it's because we British view the sea as a prosaic necessity.

Having spent a pleasant fortnight in Les Sables-d'Olonne for the Vendée Globe race start, I could see why the French attract so many visitors for this race. Over a million came to see the boats, enjoy the atmosphere and provide a valuable boost to the local economy. Television coverage is national, the sailors are seen as gladiators and the sponsors derive valuable publicity as a result.

The boats, the sailors and their support crews and sponsors are not the only attraction – ashore there is a large village full of free attractions, covering not just the race and it history but many other aspects of the sea.

The French see the sea in a far more romantic fashion than we British, as befits a nation that has land boundaries and did not have to depend on the sea. Being islanders we tend to see the sea more prosaically; we view it in practical terms as a way to connect with the rest of the world because, without ships, we are isolated. We have not been successfully invaded for nearly 1,000 years and the only reason William the Conqueror was able to cross the Channel with his army was because Harold did not have a navy. So, the sea is, for the British, an essential moat for our defence and a vital link with the rest of the world. The sea is the source of a huge proportion of our imports and exports, and a place where some six per cent of us enjoy our boating pastime.

British seamen were famously described by Lady Astor as "half the scum of the world". The French see their seamen in a far more romantic light.

This all adds up to a greater national interest in sailing events among the French. Instead of a small column tucked away in the sporting pages of the newspapers, in France sailing is front-page news. This year's Vendée got off to the usual start, by which I mean boats started dropping out quickly. Two had early collisions with fishing boats off the coast of Portugal, which calls into question the electronic watch-keeping methods in use. The only positive in these cases is that the boats are now built so lightly they are unlikely to do more than superficial damage to a sturdy fishing boat.

A keel has broken, a mast has gone, electronic steering has failed and there's been a collision with a floating object – it has all been, sadly, rather predictable, with 35 per cent of the fleet falling out within two weeks – before the boats even reach the Roaring Forties.

The collision with something in the water is unfortunate, and not much can be done about that, but you would have thought other failures could have been avoided before the race with sufficient working up.

The Vendée Globe is a very hard race, probably the toughest challenge in sport. Less than 100 people have sailed non-stop around the world solo whereas more than 500 people have gone into space.

So it is not surprising that there is a high drop-out rate. Over the years the average number of finishers in this race is almost exactly 50 per cent of the starters, though four years ago there were 66 per cent.

The worry is that the boats are being pared dangerously to achieve lightness. That is fine when you are sailing close to the coast or even crossing the Atlantic in a controlled race, but it might be dangerous, even foolhardy, if there is a bad summer in the Southern Hemisphere. The Southern Ocean weather has not been that bad for some years now, and, rather like the years before the 1979 Fastnet Race when conditions were calm, people can be lulled into a false sense of security.

In the Whitbread in 1977, Jules Verne in 1993 and 1994 and Velux 5-Oceans Race in 2006-7, I never saw waves as large as I saw in *Suhaili* in 1968-9. Luck perhaps, but our weather has become less predictable in the intervening years and I am not a believer in going to sea depending on luck.

LERWICK

It's the festivities during stopovers as much
as the sailing that make the Round Britain and
Ireland two-hander a gem of a race, and nowhere
are things more festive than Lerwick.

I have participated in the Round Britain and Ireland Race seven times.
Organised by the Plymouth-based Royal Western Yacht Club of England,
the two-hander is one of our classic yacht races. The British Isles seem
purpose-designed to sail round and this event not only takes you
around our varied coastline, it provides a chance to enjoy some fantastic
destinations en route.

Officially, the 48-hour pauses permitted under the event rules are
to recover from racing and effect repairs. Unofficially, they provide an
opportunity to get to know the other contestants, which builds up the
sort of wonderful atmosphere and camaraderie not afforded by non-stop
races.

Usually everyone is too busy before the start of an event and rushes
away after the finish, so the opportunity for socialising among sailors is
limited. But away from the stress of the start in the stopping ports, you
have time to get to know your fellow competitors in a more relaxed mood.

One feature of previous Round Britains was that in Lerwick, capital of
the Shetland Islands, the crew of each boat was adopted by a local family,
usually through the Lerwick Boating Club. They met you on arrival,
took you to their home, provided a bath, woke you up when you almost
inevitably fell asleep in the water as the salt soaked away and warmth

penetrated aching muscles, and gave you a huge meal and – bliss! – a bed.

You awoke to find your clothes laundered and plans laid for the rest of your stay in the town. It is little wonder that we all loved Lerwick.

My happy memories of Lerwick include sailing with Bob Fisher on *Barracuda*, trying to turn our boat around, so we were ready to depart during the early hours with minimum fuss. The wind was making it difficult and lines had to be moved fast.

Standing on the quay, I asked everyone to back away from the edge, so I had a clear run when I took a line down very quickly to another bollard. Everyone moved except one chap, who just looked at me and ignored my signals. At that moment, Bob let the line go. I ran. The man was in my way, so I just cannoned past him and secured the line to make our boat safe.

The unfortunate bystander picked himself up to hear Bob ask me: "What position did you play?"

"Flanker," I responded.

"Well, I wish I had been behind you when I was playing scrum-half," Bob replied, which I did not think was very diplomatic. Twenty years later I would like to apologise to that spectator, but in fairness, I did ask him to get clear and that line had to be moved quickly or our boat would have crashed into other competitors.

On another occasion I received a ransom demand. I had left my jumper in Cork on the only occasion I have tried to play golf. Euan Southby Tailyour, who was following on, agreed to bring it for me. In Lerwick, I received his note: if I did not leave a bottle of whisky there, I would receive an arm of my jumper as a ball of wool.

In the race office I found a parcel for Euan from London tailors Gieves & Hawkes. Ignoring rules about interference with Her Majesty's mail, I borrowed it, removed the brand new yachting cap inside and replaced it with a note suggesting the Red Cross could arrange an exchange. Both hostages were later returned unharmed.

In 1974 on OXO cube of a fisherman came into the clubhouse and. after a few beers, declared that all yachtsmen were cream puffs. Many of us were upset at this, so we sorted it out with a pull-ups challenge on the roof beams. He faded at 44.

Four years later I was back and guess who was waiting for me to get his revenge when we arrived. He had clearly been in intensive training as he even had muscles in his earlobes! At the time I was recovering from shingles that had taken two stone (14kgs) from my weight and could barely manage a single press-up, so I told him he had won. Bless him, he really wanted a competition, but I was just not up to him this time around.

With happy memories like these you can see why I rate the Round Britain so highly. The maximum boat length is now set at 50ft, partly to keep down costs but also to ensure the race is for those without big budgets. This is real competition, one about ability not budgets. Amen to that.

CENTRAL LONDON

The start of the Clipper Race at London's Tower Bridge required 12 yachts to parade in perfect formation while dodging river-buses, tour boats and tugs. What could possibly go wrong?

Central London is not the easiest place to start a yacht race despite the appeal of Tower Bridge as an iconic backdrop. We did it in the 1970s for a February race downriver to the Erith Yacht Club, but the boats were smaller and the spectator boats didn't get much custom from tourists in winter.

So, when I asked if I could do a parade of 12 70ft yachts at the beginning of September, passing through the lifting bridge then downriver as a prelude to the 2013-14 Clipper Round the World Race, there was a certain amount of tooth-sucking from the Port of London Authority (PLA).

They made the valid point that this section of the River Thames is the busiest waterway in the UK. Not only is it plied by boats for tourists and the river-bus most of the time, there are also tugs with barges coming downriver with the ebb and unable to manoeuvre easily.

Eventually the PLA agreed if we came in and out straight away, but Transport for London was not prepared to keep the bridge open for the 11 minutes we estimated our parade would take. Or rather they would so long as we paid through the nose to have the streets closed and diversions in place.

So, we dropped it and went for a Plan B created by race director Justin Taylor. We would put four boats through the bridge, then it would close to river traffic for half an hour to allow road traffic through, then our boats would exit. Fine, but what do we do with our other eight boats in the meantime? We could not keep them in St Katharine Docks marina because there would be insufficient water for them to exit via the lock by that time, so they had to be in the river nearby.

Our solution – to create a holding area downriver by Shadwell where they could circle slowly and avoid other river traffic – was accepted by the PLA, but now we had some timing problems. To allow around 120,000 family, friends and spectators to see the fleet before it set off around the world, we needed boats to parade up to the bridge. Four of them went through, the other eight peeled off down to Shadwell.

Getting the parade reformed for the passage downriver required the eight yachts to come back up precisely as the four came through the bridge. Having these large yachts in a river that was filled with pleasure craft was dangerous enough, but to effect this precision was going to need a miracle.

We briefed the owners and skippers of the pleasure craft, river bus, the PLA and, of course, the Clipper skippers and crossed our fingers. If it worked it would be brilliant, but there was plenty of scope for difficulties, especially from boats outside our control. Fortunately, we had the PLA and river police on hand to deal with emergencies, so went ahead.

The speed of the eight had to be carefully co-ordinated. The boats would be in line at boat-length intervals, so a change in speed by the leader could open up that gap, or, more problematically, close it to the point where the boats were almost hitting each other.

It was a far from easy task for the skippers; they had to monitor the VHF to adjust speed together, avoid other traffic and avoid hitting each other, but keep the line formation. As the last boat came under the open Tower Bridge and approached level with St Katharine Docks, the first of the eight was in place and crossed from the north to the south side to fall into place. They did it to the second and I was immensely proud of them.

We could not have raced these large yachts downriver safely and we did not try. We took them to Queenborough for the night, a lovely safe anchorage with some moorings at the entrance to the River Medway, to avoid tired skippers having to navigate around the forelands and through Dover Strait.

Then next morning we crossed to the Essex side and set up a start line with the aid of the Benfleet Yacht Club and the Queenborough Harbour Trust and Sheppey Sailing Club, and sent them on their way. At 09.30 hrs the start gun fired and they were off round the world.

Making Waves

The real lives of sporting heroes on, in & under the water

One Man's Voyage in Pursuit of Freedom

A weekend sailor's voyage in 50 day sails

The lives and tragic loss of remarkable sailors who never returned

The first Indian solo circumnavigation under sail

GOLDEN Lily

Asia's first dinghy sailing gold medallist

Understanding a
NAUTICAL CHART

- How to read and interpret essential chart information
- Establish the true accuracy of your charts
- An invaluable chart table resource for all leisure sailors & mariners
- Includes the UKHO 5011 Symbols and Abbreviataions used on Admiralty Paper charts

Learn the Nautical
RULES OF THE ROAD

- The Essential Guide to the COLREGs
- For yachtsmen and professional mariners
- Access to free online tests
- Ideal for exam preparation

Available to buy from all good bookshops, websites and direct from
www.fernhurstbooks.com.

 **FERNHURST** BOOKS

On 22 April 1969, Sir Robin Knox-Johnston secured his place in the history books, becoming the first person to sail solo, and non-stop around the globe when he and his 32-ft ketch, *Suhaili*, returned first into Falmouth, UK after an incredible 312 days at sea in the ***Sunday Times*** Golden Globe Race.

Unsatisfied at achieving this awesome adventure feat for himself, Sir Robin believes strongly that everyone should have the opportunity to experience the challenge and sheer exhilaration of ocean racing. Twenty years ago he achieved this aim when he established The Clipper Round the World Yacht Race, the only event on the planet which trains non-professionals to follow his experiences.

Since then, approximately 5,000 novices have been transformed into ocean racing yachtsmen and women. They choose to cross single oceans or, go ahead and complete the ultimate bucket list challenge, a circumnavigation of our remarkable planet, just like Sir Robin.

Fewer people have raced a yacht around the globe than have climbed Mount Everest, and as Sir Robin says: "You only have one life, paint it in bright colours not pastel shades."

Life is too short, so what are you waiting for? If you want to be part of one of the biggest endurance challenges of the natural world, and experience something truly remarkable on the race of your life, visit **www.clipperroundtheworld.com** to find out more.